BEYOND THE IVORY TOWER
THE UNIVERSITY IN THE NEW MILLENNIUM

BEYOND THE IVORY TOWER
THE UNIVERSITY IN THE NEW MILLENNIUM

Edited by

ANGELA HOEY-HEFFRON
JAMES HEFFRON

Published in association with

CONVOCATION
OF
THE NATIONAL UNIVERSITY OF IRELAND

MERCIER PRESS

MERCIER PRESS
5 French Church Street, Cork
and
16 Hume Street, Dublin 2

Trade enquiries to COLUMBA MERCIER DISTRIBUTION,
55a Spruce Avenue, Stillorgan Industrial Park, Blackrock, Dublin

© Covocation of the National University of Ireland, 2001

ISBN: 1 85635 377 X

10 9 8 7 6 5 4 3 2 1

Printed in Ireland by Colour Books Ltd.

CONTENTS

FOREWORD

The quest for knowledge is a never-ending and enriching pursuit. Despite commercial and business imperatives new knowledge is sought with fervour and fascination in the universities of the world. Although the role of the university is in a great state of flux there is little doubt that the university is still the foremost institution in the systematic and serendipitous intellectual and physical exploration of the universe while maintaining its links with the great repositories of learning and knowledge.

The new millennium is a timely occasion to examine where the university is going in a period of the most rapid change in human history. To this end the Convocation of the National University of Ireland endeavoured to assemble a group of interested and able intellectuals to record their perceptions of the idea of the university. Convocation sought authors not only from the four NUI universities (University College Cork; University College Dublin, National University of Ireland Galway and National University of Ireland Maynooth) but also from the three other statutory universities of the State, the University of Dublin (Trinity College Dublin), the University of Limerick and Dublin City University. Authors were encouraged to express their own independent views limited only by the space available.

Many are not familiar with the meaning of Convocation. It is a legislative or deliberative assembly of a university. Not all universities have formal convocations but the Convocation of the National University of Ireland is the statutory graduate representative body of the University. It is one of the authorities of the University in continuous existence since the issue of its charter on 2 December 1908. The powers of Convocation are enshrined in the charter, in the Irish Universities Act 1908 and in the 1997 Universities Act. These are:

- To elect the Chancellor of the University.
- To elect eight of its own members as its representatives on the Senate of the University.
- To elect three of its members to Seanad Éireann (State Senate).
- To discuss and pronounce an opinion on any matter whatsoever relating to the University.
- To make representations to the Senate on any matter affecting the University.
- To make regulations governing the University's proceedings.

All graduates of the National University of Ireland, including honorary graduates, are members of Convocation. National University of Ireland graduates include all the graduates of University College Cork, University College Dublin, National University of Ireland Galway, National University of Ireland Maynooth, and graduates from the Royal College of Surgeons since they have been granted degrees from University College Dublin from 1977; graduates from St Angela's College of Education, Sligo from 1978 and from the National College of Art and Design from 1996, Shannon College of Hotel Management from 2000 and Institute of Public Administration from 2001.

The editors wish to thank the members of the Council of Convocation for their unanimous approval and encouragement of the project.

DOLPHINS AND THE GOOD LIFE
A PHILOSOPHICAL CHALLENGE TO THE UNIVERSITY

Patrick Riordan, SJ

The widespread interest in animal behaviour coupled with the ever more vocal agitation on behalf of animal rights has made teachers of philosophy cautious when presenting traditional understandings of humans as rational in comparison with other animals. That certain species of animals are highly intelligent, that they can communicate and that they are capable of learning is evident from the close observation of their behaviour recorded for us in the nature films that are a staple feature of the television programme. Accordingly, philosophers have begun to explore questions about animal thinking, whether beliefs can be ascribed to animals, whether they require a language in order to think, or whether they can think and form intentions without relying on concepts. Alasdair MacIntyre has begun his recent book with a review of such explorations, with special interest in dolphins.[1] However, MacIntyre's main interest remains the human, and in usual philosophical fashion he draws attention to the similarities between humans and dolphins in order to highlight the significant differences. Among the similarities he notes is the great vulnerability of the young, and their depen-

Patrick Riordan, SJ, was President of The Milltown Institute of Theology and Philosophy 1997–2000. He is Senior Lecturer in the Faculty of Philosophy, specialising in political philosophy. He is the author of A Politics of the Common Good *(Dublin: Institute of Public Administration, 1996).*

dence on nurture and education. Many of the threats to the young of both species are similar, whether they are threats to survival or threats to the achievement of a flourishing existence in maturity. The major differences are in what constitutes flourishing for both species. 'Dolphins can flourish without being able to argue with and learn from others about dolphin flourishing. Humans at times cannot flourish without arguing with others and learning from them about human flourishing.'[2]

It is part of doing well as a human being that one enters into discussion with others about what is worthwhile pursuing. What is good for us, at this juncture in our history, or what is good for me to pursue now, being the person I am with the qualities that I have, are basic questions that recur for mature adults. How adequately they handle and answer these questions will determine whether they succeed in flourishing as human beings. Accordingly, unlike young dolphins, young humans must learn to be practical reasoners, and that means that they must grow in understanding themselves by having to deliberate about their good. MacIntyre's main focus in this book is on the qualities required by people as they engage in the relevant search and discussion about their good, namely, the virtues. This book therefore is in sequence with earlier works to which it is to some extent a correction.[3] The emphasis on dependency, the exploration of the implications of the fact that we are all at some stages of our lives completely dependent on others, and some of us, by virtue of handicap, are always dependent, adds a new perspective. The characterisation of human society and the elaboration of what is involved in identifying and pursuing our good, are affected.

WHAT IS THE POINT OF UNIVERSITY EDUCATION?

If the good life, if human flourishing requires participation in discourse about the human good, might we expect the university to have some function in relation to this activity? Elsewhere I have discussed the purposes of the university as elaborated in the Universities Act 1997. It is remarkable not only that there is so little in the act's specification of the purposes of the university that refers to human flourishing and the good life, but also that there has been so little political debate precisely about what it is we expect from our universities.

Section 12 of the act places the advancement of knowledge and research and the promotion of learning at the top of the list of objectives of the university, although without intending to give it priority.[5] This is reassuring for some, given the fear that the demands of the economy and the labour market's need for skilled workers have become too influential in setting the agenda for education. However, the act gives no clear reason why knowledge and research are valuable for our society. There is a related tension between the vocational and the educational functions of the university as outlined in this section of the act. The training of students in the skills and expertise required in the range of professions from engineering to teaching is a recognised part of the university's role. Everyone can see easily enough the rationale behind the training of good technicians, scientists, lawyers, doctors and architects, but how do we explain the importance of educating good people and good citizens? The latter cannot be the object of certification, and yet a society, which is organised politically in a democratic system, must be at least as concerned about the quality of its voters as it is about the quality of its pharmacists. After all, it is the discourse that they will

11

engage in about the goods worth pursuing which will shape the life of society.

An innovation in the 1997 act is the assertion of the university's responsibility towards society. Against any tendency there might be for the university to become an ivory tower, comfortably isolated from the society around it, the act imposes on the university the obligation 'to promote the cultural and social life of society'. Admittedly, this is qualified with a clause which allows the diversity of the university's traditions to be fostered and respected. In a further listed objective, in which the promotion of the Irish language is given special place, the obligation to preserve and promote the distinctive cultures of Ireland is imposed. But which cultures are to be preserved and promoted? All which can be identified as existing in Ireland, including the culture of political violence?

Recognition of the diversity of cultures seems impossible without at the same time facing the fact that cultures can be in conflict with one another. Different cultural and political traditions view one another as opponents and the ideals and purposes they pursue are mutually incompatible. And yet, the act speaks as if it were possible for the university to promote all cultures. How ought the university, and indeed society in general, deal with this social and political reality of conflicted diversity? What contribution can the university make to society's handling of conflict?

There is a delightful irony in the way in which the act identifies the cultivation of independent critical thinking amongst students as a purpose of the university, while at the same time requiring the university to 'support and contribute to the realisation of national economic and social development'. It appears

as if the university is simply to accept the goals of national economic and social development having been set by some other entity, the government perhaps, and to contribute to the national endeavour in a supportive capacity. But could its contribution be critical? Is it part of its function to provide independent critical thinking on the direction and goals of economic and social development?

This brief review of one section of the Universities Act highlights real issues that affect not only the university itself but also the quality of our political life. These issues are good examples (although not exhaustive) of the questions about the goods which MacIntyre thinks young humans must learn to pursue in discussion with others if they are to flourish. However, MacIntyre, in this latest book, as in earlier works, denies that the good life, in which the discourse about the good is constitutive, is attainable through the politics of the sovereign nation state. What is more, he has also questioned the ability of the contemporary university to provide the forum for the conducting of the debate around such questions. This is a radical challenge and deserves consideration.

MacIntyre on the Crisis of the University

In an earlier book, MacIntyre had argued that the contemporary university has failed to articulate for itself what it is about, and this is the reason why it has not been able to provide an adequate answer to those who have challenged it from commercial and politically-motivated perspectives.[6] MacIntyre's explanation is that the universities' failure is due to the exclusion from their ambit of the very disciplines which would have addressed the relevant questions. The exclusion of a certain type of moral philosophy and of committed theology has deprived the university community of the disciplines, which traditionally have pursued the questions of the good and the ordering of goods. Without these intellectual resources, the academic community is handicapped in its response to the pressures to serve the needs of the economy and to cater for the interests of the politically powerful.

MacIntyre offers us a history of the university, noting the pre-liberal and the liberal stages already experienced, and outlining the university of the future to which he aspires. This schedule mirrors the history of moral philosophy to which he devotes his trilogy. His basic thesis is that contemporary moral discourse is characterised by disputes without resolution, in which conflicting positions are articulated on the basis of incommensurable premises and principles. That such debates are interminable lends plausibility to the emotivist thesis that moral language has to do with the expression of feeling, and is not rational in any proper sense.[7] The popularity of the emotivist stance is an understandable reaction to the failure of the attempt to provide rational grounding for morality in the absence of agreement on the human *telos*, the good life for human beings. MacIntyre argues that despite the failure to construct agreement on the basis of some rational ground, and despite the prevalence of an emotivist view of moral language, the academic life of the modern university proceeds *as if* there were in fact a stance of neutral rationality, independent of commitment to a view of the good in some tradition. Teachers in various disciplines typically introduce students to rival fundamental positions and train them to discuss the pros and cons of each. The assumption behind this typical academic approach is that there is a neutral, rational stance, from

14

which the committed positions are to be judged, and this assumption persists in animating academic life, despite the obvious experience that the debates, in the terms in which they are couched, are interminable. It seems that the failure to realise the dreams of the Enlightenment thinkers from Hobbes to Kant has in no measure diminished the power of this myth to sustain the academic endeavour. The persistence of the assumption of neutral rationality makes the modern university inhospitable to a committed engagement with questions of the good.

An answer to the critics who want to know why resources should be diverted to university education, and why the university should not have to pay its way or at least prove its usefulness in commercial terms, would depend on some scale of values in which the goods of finance and commerce were relativised. The defence of the university in reply to such challenge would be by appeal to some specific account of how human goods are to be ordered. The position of the goods associated with the practices of enquiry, and indeed of the other goods associated with the activities of the university, would have to be located within that ordering of goods. The defence cannot be provided, however, because 'the absence from the university of any form of rational enquiry providing such a systematic understanding of how goods are to be ordered inevitably deprives the university of any adequate response to its external critics'.[8]

It is obvious that MacIntyre would like to provide the university with the kind of defence which it requires, and so he advocates that the engaged dialectical disciplines of theology and moral philosophy be restored to the university. In contrast to the preceding forms of the university, (1) the pre-liberal university, characterised by constrained agreement, and (2) the lib-

15

eral university striving for unconstrained agreement, MacIntyre envisages the university of the future as a place of constrained disagreement. What is needed is a forum in which fundamental moral and religious conflicts are admitted to a central place in the curriculum. Participation in conflict would be required and students would be initiated into conflict. The scholar would have a double role: (i) participate in conflict as the protagonist of a particular point of view, advance enquiry from within that particular point of view, and enter into controversy with other rival standpoints; and at the same time (ii) uphold and order the ongoing conflicts so that the university is sustained as an arena of conflict in which the most fundamental type of moral and theological disagreement is recognised.

SCHOOLS FOR DOLPHINS?

Is the intelligence of the human different from that of the dolphin? If, as MacIntyre has suggested, what is distinctive about humans is their need to enter into discussion with one another about their good in order to be able to achieve that good, then a key element of human life in society will be the maintenance of the conditions for public discourse, and a key element in the education of the young will be their initiation into the methods of questioning and debate about the good. As an institution, significant both for the quality of public debate, and for the quality of education given to the young, the university has a crucial function. But perhaps its self-understanding now is such that it has made itself incapable of performing the necessary roles in the pursuit of the good. And perhaps the position accorded to it by the legislators in the 1997 act is one that makes it subservient to someone else's idea of the good. If either or both of these suggestions is the case, perhaps MacIntyre's analysis and proposals offer the university an opportunity for a renewed role in the new century.

NOTES

1: MacIntyre, Alasdair, *Dependent Rational Animals. Why Human Beings Need the Virtues*, Open Court, Chicago, 1999.

2: Ibid., pp. 67–8.

3: MacIntyre, Alasdair, *After Virtue* University of Notre Dame Press, Indiana, 1984; *Whose Justice? Which Rationality?*, Duckworth, London, 1988; and *Three Rival Versions of Moral Enquiry*, Duckworth, London, 1990.

4: O'Riordan, P., 'The Common Good of a Pluralist Society', in *Social Policy in Ireland. Principles, Practice and Problems* (eds. Healy, Seán & Reynolds, Brigid) Oak Tree Press, Dublin, 1998, pp. 43–58.

5: *The Universities Act 1997*, Stationery Office, Dublin, 1997, p. 62.

6: MacIntyre, *Three Rival Versions of Moral Enquiry* (n. 3), pp. 221–222.

7: MacIntyre, *After Virtue* (n. 3), chapter 3.

8: MacIntyre, *Three Rival Versions of Moral Enquiry* (n. 3), p. 227.

THE MYTH OF ACADEMIC FREEDOM AND UNIVERSITY AUTONOMY

John Kelly

Recent decades have seen major changes in the role of university education throughout the world. Many of these developments are in marked contrast to the ivory tower ethos of the traditional universities so that inevitably, there is conflict between the old and the new, which varies in substance and intensity in different parts of the world, depending on local traditions and politics. Whilst it is a non-uniform and somewhat confused scenario, it would appear that there is a convergence whereby the more traditional universities, however reluctantly and painstakingly, are dismantling sections of their ivory towers, brick by brick, whilst the newer more vocational institutions are seeking peer recognition and academic respectability in the greater university world. It is, however, a turbulent scene where the process dynamics are driven by huge increases in student numbers in many countries, where student participation in higher education, as measured by the percentage of the 18 year old age cohort,

Professor John Kelly obtained the BE and PhD degrees in Chemical Engineering from University College Dublin. He has served on the Governing Body of UCD and the Senate of the National University of Ireland for many years. In addition to publishing over 100 technical and professional articles in national and international journals, he has co-authored a book and was founding editor of the journal Industry and Higher Education. *He is a former Chairman of HEDCO and of the EU Academic Consultative Group on SOCRATES and, most recently, of the new Irish Research Council for Science, Engineering and Technology.*

has moved from the *elite* phase of less than 5 per cent in the pre 1950s, to the *mass* phase of 30 per cent to 50 per cent in recent times, and which appears to be continuing onwards to a *universal* phase of 50 per cent plus.

There can be no doubt that the role of the contemporary university in modern society has changed utterly from its origins, so that the vital role which the traditional university has had in the formation of the cultural and spiritual values of our world will be diminished or lost entirely in the headlong stampede towards vocationalism in the new higher education ethos.

The university world is, of course, an organic system, inhabited by very intelligent people whose driving force is intellectual discovery and creativity so that it is not surprising that it is in a continual state of intellectual turbulence. The changes of recent decades from say, the middle of the twentieth century, have been on a macro scale, so that there is evidence to support the thesis that the spiritual and cultural ethos established over the preceding 1,000 years is under severe threat.

The emerging functions of the universities, which are inevitably interrelated, are considered under the following headings:

- student numbers
- curricula development
- quality assessment and accreditation
- university governance
- teaching and research
- academic staff
- university autonomy and academic freedom

Driven largely by national economic development strategies, the student participation rate in higher education in almost all countries is rising every year so that, in Ireland and in many other countries, it is now in excess of 40 per cent in the various third-level institutions of higher education. The demand for skilled graduates in the marketplace is being met by the universities which have effectively become the powerhouses of industrial development throughout the world, and they would appear to be doing a fairly good job of it. Thus third-level education, with a growing emphasis on vocationalism, is lining up in direct succession to the primary and secondary level education sectors as the normal and expected route for all young persons today, male and female.

This increase in student numbers has inevitably caused a reduction in academic standards at undergraduate levels, so that the pursuit of academic excellence is shifting from the undergraduate to the postgraduate levels in teaching as well as in research. This has been the experience in America for a long time now, indeed since the Second World War, but it is quite a new experience in Europe and it is growing but hasn't quite established itself yet. This new function of the universities to have to educate larger numbers of students at somewhat lower standards than heretofore presents difficulties to all third-level institutions, but perhaps more so for the older universities who have had it so good for so long with the elite of most intelligent students.

It has been a particular feature of academic life over recent decades that disciplines keep sub-dividing themselves into smaller units and that some of these units develop further to become fully fledged disciplines with degrees awarded as part of the regular university calendar. With the extraordinary growth in research in all university disciplines in recent times, and in particular in inter-disciplinary research, it is hardly surprising that successful researchers will, with the enthusiastic collaboration of their international colleagues, stake out their own new academic domain, laying claim to its vital importance in the larger discipline of which it is a part.

My own field of engineering is a good example of this expansion of disciplines where some 100 years ago there were only two types of engineering, civil and military, whereas now there must be about 40 separate disciplines offered for degree status in the university world. But in this growth process, others have come and gone or have become subsumed into another discipline with a marginally different emphasis and title. It is a tough game, and many fledgling disciplines have not survived in the treacherous seas of academic survival.

Many traditional academics view the proliferation of new degrees as a forest fire out of control. In the past, American universities were often derided by traditionalists in Europe for their recognition of 'funny' degrees in so-called disciplines such as Dance, Mortuary Science and Nursing, whilst the European universities were always more staid and conservative in their curriculum development, and none more so that the British. Now it would seem that the situation has been reversed, especially in the UK, once the pillar of academic conservatism and traditional

21

good sense. It has been reported recently that there are over 40,000 different degrees on offer in their universities. Degrees in Surfing, Knitting, Golf Course Management and Asian Culture and Cuisine (jokingly and most unfairly derided in some sectors of the UK media as 'how to cook a curry'), are now on offer to new students alongside the traditional options of Law, Medicine, English Literature, etc. Most of these new courses are to be found in the Business and Commerce faculties and seem to be very popular with the students who, voting with their feet in large numbers, are deserting the 'hard' disciplines of Science and Engineering in favour of these new courses – a situation which is regarded as most serious for the future health of the Science and Technology industry in the United States as well as in Europe.

Critics of these developments in curricula, and as is normal in academe with any innovation there are many, throw up their hands in horror at these new courses which are offered mostly, but not exclusively, in the new polytechnic-promoted universities, describing them as quasi-academic and vacuous, bolstered in absurd ways with academic padding so as to stretch them artificially over a three or four year degree programme. On the other hand, critics of these critics call them academic snobs, intellectual dinosaurs who are out of tune with the demands of the students and the industrial marketplace. Indeed, it would seem that the marketplace is effectively in charge of the admission policies of the UK university world and that the traditional academics with their cap and gown and Socratic ethos have been consigned to the overflowing bin of academic history. Similar developments are in evidence in many other European universities but the UK is clearly leading the way.

QUALITY ASSURANCE AND ACCREDITATION

A major development of this past decade is the increasing emphasis on quality assurance (QA) and the need for accreditation of individual courses and of whole institutions. With the growth of higher education, the demand has come from governments and from the marketplace for measures of assurance that the quality of the courses and degrees that are on offer is of a suitably high standard. In short, the consumer needs to be assured of the various products that are available in the market. Whilst no one will make the argument that quality is not important, the traditional universities and professors will challenge this huge new emphasis on quality, asking the question: *what is wrong with the system we have had for generations, where the market knows which are the good institutions and which are not?* Traditionalists will also ask, *what is wrong with the principle of* Caveat Emptor *in higher education?* Let the buyer beware, which is the understanding on which you buy a second hand car – but enrolling for an MBA is not the same as buying a used car, and especially with the increase in private universities, the need for quality control to protect the marketplace has become very necessary. Thus it is that the whole business of QA has become a major player in the HE world, with many professional organisations springing up all over the place and many conferences and seminars being held to discuss the optimum strategy and procedures for both universities and national governments. At the coal face in the university departments, academics are not all that happy with the intrusive nature of this new development where they have to fill out forms, entertain visiting assessment panels and have observers sitting in on their lectures. Again, this is part of the culture built into the newer universities but some traditional

23

universities find great difficulty with this whole new business. It is an evolving new ethos where the structures are not yet finalised and where there is still a strong reaction in many university circles against the more intrusive and bureaucratic aspects of the QA business, especially accreditation.

UNIVERSITY GOVERNANCE

It used to be in the 'good old days' that universities were fiercely proud of their ivory tower status and were completely independent of outside influences from the business world or from regional or national governments, which indeed had little or no interest anyway in what was going on behind their high walls – that is excepting the Church which, in mediaeval Europe, had enormous influence and control over the academic and management ethos of the universities.

Universities were, according to the German Meiners 'a manifestation of the powerful progress of the spirit', and according to the American Haskins 'the ancient and universal company of scholars', or according to the Englishman Newman 'a seat of wisdom, a light of the world, a minister of the faith, an *alma mater* of the rising generation' or some may prefer Marx 'institutions – founded in order to train the persons who are needed to maintain the ruling-class domination'. For the vast majority of the universities in the world today, those days are gone forever and the universities are venues where most young people spend some years getting trained and educated so that they may get gainful employment in the world outside – and the universities are dependent, either totally or partially, on external financing from governments or elsewhere. Thus, it is that governments are demanding to have some role in the governance of the uni-

24

versities they are financing. Universities are seen to be a vital and essential component in a successful national economic development strategy – too vital indeed to be left entirely to the discretion of those 'egghead' academics.

In some cases in the more traditional universities, this intrusion is being resisted with passion and public rhetoric particularly in the very old universities where for over 400 years they have never had outside representation on their governing senate. The slogan 'he who pays the piper calls the tunes' may be anathema to the traditional university world but this battle is surely being lost throughout the world as governments are contributing huge sums to the university world to support the increases in student numbers and are obliged to their taxpayers to ensure that their funds are well spent.

The expansion of the university world has, for the most part, been financed from public funds by enthusiastic governments believing with much validity that it is money well spent for the future industrial development of their countries. In return, governments everywhere are demanding much tighter financial accountability by the universities. Gone too are the days when a university was given a lump sum each year loosely based on their student numbers and on what it got last year – with the understanding that it had a high degree of freedom to transfer those funds between teaching, research and administration as it saw necessary during that year with a very low level of accountability. Now the normal arrangement is that all government funds allocated are earmarked with little or no degrees of freedom to transfer them from one domain to another. Governments are also demanding a more vocational emphasis in the curricula, often leading to some level of control such as they have in the other primary and secondary sectors of the national education system. Much has been written and discussed, within and outside academe, on the need for what Professor Van Ginkel calls the 'golden mean' of government control in university governance. Too much control of academic decisions by governments will kill the intellectual and creative spirit of the universities whilst on the other hand, the sums are simply too great to allow the academic world to spend them without any reference to national economic priorities. It is a major and vital debate in all our countries.

The role of industry in university governance is also of importance in the emerging functions of the university world. The newer universities with strong vocational emphasis and mission statements linking them with the local and national industrial worlds, have no difficulty in this area, indeed they welcome it. The links which they have outside often leads to the involvement of representatives of industry in many academic areas such as curricula development, teaching, university-industry co-operation and, of course, research.

It would be foolish to attempt to generalise on this topic and it would certainly be incorrect to claim that the newer universities are always more open and enthusiastic to outside involvement in university governance, whether administrative or academic, than the older more traditional universities. There are many examples of the opposite being the case. It would be true to note however that the statutes and structures of the newer institutions are generally designed in order to promote a high level of outside involvement whereas that is not the case with the older universities.

Whilst all academics will subscribe to the thesis *that freedom in research and teaching is the fundamental principle of university life,* no one can deny that the freedom (call it no. 1) to select the topics for research and, to an increasing extent, for teaching has been largely lost by the university world to outside authorities, whilst the freedom (call it no. 2) to select and deliver the specific coursework or research for those *nominated* topics still survives within the universities, with the control most often with the individual academic, department or faculty. This distinction between the two freedoms is not clear in the 'Magna Carta of European Universities', signed in Bologna in 1988, which stated: '– to meet the needs of the world around it, its research and teaching must be morally and intellectually independent of all political authority and economic power'. It would be a bold academic who would disagree with that statement, but where a government is paying all the bills, it will understandably not permit a university to establish a major new teaching programme in, say electronic engineering with associated laboratories and staffing, without a persuasive case being made, and agreed to, with regard to national economic priorities and the financial as well as the educational implications of such an initiative.

In the curriculum area, courses typically at postgraduate level are often designed and delivered in collaboration with local industries and/or local government. Such courses are often part-time and increasingly are using satellite or web communication techniques in their teaching methods so as to cater for those in full-time employment or who, for whatever reason, do not find it convenient to physically attend on campus.

Again, it is not possible or wise to generalise, but it may be that in teaching, the new universities have a more liberal approach to such procedures as part-time teaching, adjunct professors, the use of student assessments for course and professor evaluations, but this is a personal observation from limited observation. Likewise with the use of a modular-based credit system in teaching and semes-terisation which are new to most European universities, the older universities would seem to be somewhat slower to adopt these and their associated continuous assessment procedures – the supermarket shopping basket approach as to which it is sometimes disdainfully referred.

The use of satellite communications and other distance learning technologies are still evolving and have yet to find their established niche in the higher education system. The developing situation of the international MBA is worth considering in this context. The top international schools in the USA and in Europe have in general shied away from going on-line because of their concerns over course quality and the possible damage to their reputation – and the conservative philosophy of 'if it ain't broken, don't fix it' has many followers. The traditional MBA ethos relies on group dynamics and conventional classroom teaching, both of which are difficult to replicate in the new distance learning technologies. Surprisingly the American universities have been very slow to adopt these new technologies, whereas the UK has again been the more adventurous in recent times. A major breakthrough in the UK is at Cambridge University (the prestigious Judge Institute) which has recently announced a new executive MBA supported by the internet. Though it falls well short of total online delivery, it marks a significant shift in the flagging international MBA market. The split is 35 per cent Internet and 65 per cent traditional classroom and it will be launched in September 2001 – billed as the Executive MBA for the twenty-first century.

Likewise, in the development and on-going support of the research strategy of a department, faculty or university, involvement by business persons or government representatives is common. In research more so than in the curriculum area, it is clearly a case of 'he who pays the piper calls the tunes', or at least 'he' has some consultative role, as governments and industry decide on their research priorities and fund them. Competition between the various institutions of higher education for national or international research funds is now normal practice in most countries, where the allocation of the fund priorities are not established by the universities, and the universities, traditional and modern, have no difficulty in competing for and accepting these funds.

An interesting aside to this increased external funding of research is the situation whereby outstanding professors and their research teams are now being transferred with substantial financial inducements like football players from one university to another so as to increase its chances of getting that big grant.

However it must be admitted that it is only in those few disciplines where research costs are minimal, that anything near complete freedom in research is realised, and that in the others, only freedom (no. 2) applies, and for the most part academics have accepted this situation. It is noted too that in some enlightened national and international regimes, universities have 'free money' which they have freedom to allocate to any research they choose, but in reality, the sums allocated under this heading are minuscule compared to those allocated by governments and multi-national government agencies to selected priority areas, particularly in the vast ranges of the science and technology disciplines.

ACADEMIC STAFF

Finally to the academic staff. Throughout the university world, it seems that market forces are becoming increasingly intrusive so that, with the impossibility of attracting a professor of computer science over the age of 25, to take one of many such cases, flexible appointment conditions are becoming more common. This is very difficult territory, whereby the Professor of Ancient Palaeography and Dean of the Faculty of Arts is paid $x whilst the Professor of Informatics, who is half his age, is paid $3x, with the understanding that he can consult outside for 33 per cent of his time and that he is not obliged to do any administrative work in his department, etc., etc. The newer universities seem to have more flexible procedures to meet this situation, whereas the traditional universities are often locked into a uniform system of very long standing, and change is not easy. It is, as noted above, a difficult area and no solution is offered here except to state the obvious, that the well-being of the academic staff must be the top priority in any administration, otherwise the whole system will collapse and not be a happy place to work.

UNIVERSITY AUTONOMY AND ACADEMIC FREEDOM

The terms university autonomy and academic freedom have been the war-cry of the traditional university world fighting against outside interference in the university's internal management as well as outside control of its teaching and research programmes, yet it is difficult to find a satisfactory definition of these terms which meets the current situation, and one is not attempted here. In general, the newer universities have a different interpretation of these terms from the traditional university. It is clear that those new universities which were established with an ashamedly vocational mission have no problem with outside participation on their governing senates and other university committees, academic or administrative, indeed they welcome it. With the traditional universities, this is a new concept, alien to their cultures and requiring major changes in both their philosophies and practices, and it is not easy and has been resisted with much passion and anger with cries of university autonomy.

At the heart of all these issues is the big question, what is the function of the university in our society today? All reasonable people, and there are some around, will acknowledge the validity of the arguments for changes in the traditional concept of university autonomy, but the problem is to get the formula correct. Along the scale stretching from complete autonomy and academic freedom at one end to total outside control on both academic and administrative management on the other, there are infinite possibilities, and within any country and region, different optimum arrangements will apply. Many countries have had the so-called binary system at third-level, with a clear separation of the university from the vocational educational systems, where the latter were from birth more under the direct control of the government or its government's Department of Education, and it seems to have worked quite well – except that the vocational institutes always want to become universities, the so-called academic drift, and in many countries, they have been granted that status. Whichever procedures are enforced, it would seem important for those in power to recognise the differences between institutions, and not to attempt to impose a uniform ethos and administration across them all. It just will not work. What works best, but is not favoured by the bureaucrats, is the system that allows each institution and its faculty and students develop freely and contribute in their most effective way to the cultural and economic prosperity of the country or region.

CONCLUSION

No specific conclusions are offered except to note once more that universities everywhere are being challenged by the various sectors of the society which they serve – students, industry, the taxpayers and of course the government. For centuries, they were ignored by all these sectors, but no longer. Now they are being challenged to change their traditional approaches to teaching and to research in order to meet the current more vocational needs of society. These challenges are, in general, more difficult for the older more traditional universities, than for the newer ones. For all universities everywhere, there are many and various challenges with the fast-changing functions that contemporary society is demanding of them. It is important in all of this that the vital role our universities have had throughout the centuries for the cultural and spiritual enrichment of our societies is not lost in the developing new ethos.

THE ROLE OF THE UNIVERSITY IN THE TWENTY-FIRST CENTURY

Thomas N. Mitchell

The dawn of the twenty-first century brings, in many ways, the best of times for universities, particularly in a rapidly developing, knowledge-based economy such as has emerged in Ireland in the last decade.

The teaching role of the universities is widening rapidly and will continue to grow in importance in the years ahead. The technological revolution has made knowledge and brain power the main foundations of sustainable economic development. The primary needs of a successful knowledge-based economy are expertise, combined with broad intellectual proficiency, and the capacity to go on learning. The demand for unskilled labour is therefore declining rapidly and even specialised manual skills are being superseded by intellectual skills grounded in a broad knowledge base.

This growing importance of high educational qualifications and of mental power has brought a quantum jump in the numbers seeking to enter university. At the same time those who left school without third-level or strong second-level qualifications are seeking to return as mature students, while even the highly educated are finding it necessary to pursue regular postgraduate

Thomas N. Mitchell is the immediate past Provost of Trinity College Dublin. He is a classical scholar who formerly held Chairs in the United States and at Trinity College Dublin. He has written extensively on Cicero and Roman law and politics.

training to expand their skills or keep abreast of new developments in their fields. Life-long learning has become a central feature of the knowledge age and is creating a need for a whole range of new educational services.

As education becomes the passport to material well-being and professional success, equality of access to it assumes a new importance. In the knowledge age, the gravest form of social injustice and discrimination is the failure to educate a child. The improvement of educational opportunities for the disadvantaged has become an urgent social imperative, and the creation of innovative educational services that will encourage and enable young people from disadvantaged backgrounds to achieve their academic potential will add further to the tasks and challenges facing universities in the new century.

The role of universities in research will also achieve an added importance. Innovation in knowledge-based industries requires research at the highest levels and on a grand scale. All available evidence indicates a strong correlation between industrial growth in high technology areas and levels of activity and achievement in research.

Universities are best equipped to serve the research needs of knowledge-based economies. They alone have the capacity to produce the necessary supply of well-trained researchers. They provide a broad research infrastructure and incorporate a range and concentration of expertise and mental power across the disciplines that cannot be equalled elsewhere. They can create interdisciplinary collaborations and synergies that are important ingredients in the generation of new ideas and the extension of knowledge. Researchers in universities also benefit from the stimulus of teaching and supervising graduate students and from an ethos focused on knowledge, mental effort and discovery. There is now a general acceptance in the most developed economies that research should be primarily located in universities and should take advantage of all the aids to it which the university environment provides.

The knowledge revolution will also broaden the role of universities as centres of independent thought and debate and as vital reservoirs of expertise available to serve the needs of a better-educated public with more leisure and wider intellectual interests. And it will give added importance as well to their traditional role as the chief repositories, through their libraries and museums, of old knowledge and as the custodians of our cultural and intellectual heritage.

Society will therefore become more dependent than ever on universities for a range of vital services. The consequence of this should be that universities will have greater claims on public support and investment and should be able to face the future with particular confidence and optimism.

But despite the many favourable developments, the beginning of the new century will be a testing time for the university sector. Risks to the quality of university education and to the first principles that have governed the great tradition of western education since Plato abound, and the capacity of universities in many parts of the world, and especially in Ireland, to assume the added responsibilities being imposed by the knowledge revolution remains in doubt.

I would like to highlight a number of issues, some general, some specific, that will need particular attention if universities are to safeguard their value to society and cope with the impact of the knowledge revolution.

The first issue relates to new forces that are gradually re-shaping the character of undergraduate education. The importance of high technology to industrial development, its voracious appetite for specialist skills, the preoccupation of governments and industrialists with meeting its needs and producing graduates capable of exploiting its economic potential – all of these factors are creating pressure to concentrate resources in disciplines with direct industrial application and are promoting educational programmes geared to producing technical experts with maximum speed.

A utilitarian ethos is taking hold, specialised applied skills are getting pride of place. The educational agenda is being more and more determined by forces external to the universities that are driven by pragmatic, immediate and narrowly-conceived market needs rather than by the stable first principles of education that have for so long inspired our educational ideals and underpinned the intellectual and cultural attainments of western civilisation.

Universities must recover control of their educational priorities and must determine what and how they teach by reference to tested and enduring educational values. Foremost among those must be the determination to maintain as the primary goal of undergraduate education the development of the mind and of the mental powers of speech and communication, reasoning and analysis, creativity and imagination, and moral discernment. These are the skills by which, in Cicero's words, people become fully human, *humanissimus*; they represent real brain-power and the extended mental proficiency that can be a spur to creativity and innovation, that can keep on learning and that can contribute to the true well-being of society. They are the flexible and creative skills that are most valuable and most needed in the knowledge age, and are most likely to sustain and extend the benefits that knowledge can bring.

This form of education is not quick and it is not narrow. It involves far more than specialist, vocational training. It is dependent on a broad study of core areas of knowledge, which provide the foundation for mental development and the means to an understanding of humanity and human achievement. It is dependent on an active approach to learning that is characterised by problem-solving, and by the Socratic method of using reason to test, question and explore. It is dependent on the great range of inter-disciplinary and extracurricular experiences that a university provides and, above all, it is dependent on contact and interaction with scholars who work on the forefront of their disciplines and can pass on the skills of investigation and of reasoning and analysis.

Postgraduate education can rightly concentrate on the vocational and on communicating specialist knowledge, but all undergraduate programmes, whatever the major discipline involved, should incorporate exposure to seminal areas of learning and to rigorous forms of intellectual challenge. Otherwise universities will stifle rather than stimulate the great gift of mind, and will fail in their most sacred responsibility to society, namely to foster creativity and progress informed by appreciation of the many facets of human achievement, and of the many-sided needs of a developed society.

Universities have also experienced in recent times a broader erosion of their traditional freedom to determine their educational ethos and control their overall academic decision-making. Greater preoccupation with transparency and accountability and the increasing importance of universities as the powerhouses of knowledge-based economies have led governments to intrude more directly into the detailed management of all third-level institutions. The intrusion and attempts to regulate take various forms – stringent forms of quality assurance, unlimited demands for data and detailed reporting, intensive financial scrutiny extending to private as well as public funding, restrictions on financial management and budgetary decision-making, the use of the power of the purse to set the academic agenda and promote or discourage particular academic activities.

Universities cannot, of course, claim exemption from scrutiny of their standards and systems. They must serve the public good and be responsive to public needs. They must be fully accountable for their use of public funds and must show that they give value for money. But obviously they must also have the freedom to plan and manage in accordance with their professional judgement and academic purposes, and it is clearly unwise to involve any external agency in detailed control of matters with which they can have only limited familiarity.

Universities are, besides, self-motivating institutions, whose success depends on the creativity and commitment of highly talented people who are driven by their dedication to their discipline and to scholarly investigation and discovery and who require a supportive environment that facilitates the free exercise of their talents. The heavy hand of government can be a powerful curb on the unstinting, unrecorded and, to a large extent, immeasurable and unrewarded effort that marks the best traditions of academia. These are traditions that do not flourish in highly regulated, bureaucratic systems.

But there is a still more fundamental reason why universities must never allow the state to usurp control of their educational goals or management systems. Universities have a unique value to society as centres of independent thought, untrammelled by allegiance to any particular dogma or ideology or to any political party or interest group, free without fear or hindrance to pursue truth, to question and criticise established orthodoxies, to foster debate and generate new ideas, using the tools of reasoned argument based on knowledge and insight derived from diligent research and rigorous analysis.

Universities lose that value and their essential character if they become subservient to any political forces or drift into levels of dependence that might make them an arm of government or instruments for the accomplishment of particular agendas, political, social or economic. Free societies need this disinterested pursuit of knowledge and ideas that universities alone can provide, and the academic freedom and managerial autonomy which make it possible are essential to the integrity and vitality of the university ideal that has contributed so much to our civilisation.

Other more specific difficulties will arise for universities in providing new educational services with regard to life-long learning and the expansion of educational opportunities for the disadvantaged. These difficulties will be especially formidable in Ireland, where infrastructural deficiencies and chronic underfunding, legacies of the recession-ridden 1980s, continue to impede any extension of services.

Ireland, like most Organisation for Economic Cooperation and Development countries, has invested heavily in education over the past thirty years with the result that over 80 per cent of school-leavers now complete the Leaving Certificate and 46 per cent go on to some form of third-level education.

But, while this means that the educational attainment of today's young people is high, and comparable to that of other developed countries, the situation is very different in the case of older groups, where there are still large numbers who have no third-level qualification and have not even finished upper secondary education. For example, in the age group 35–44, a group that supplies a critical element of work force needs, only 21 per cent have a third-level qualification and only 54 per cent have completed second-level. When one looks at the broader span of working years, from 25-64, only 23 per cent of that age group have completed a third-level course and only 28 per cent have completed upper secondary education. This places Ireland in the bottom third of OECD countries in overall educational attainment, and means that it has a working population whose educational qualifications are seriously deficient by the standards of other developed countries. For a country whose economy is becoming increasingly knowledge-based and whose future prosperity is dependent on building a knowledge society, this is obviously an unacceptable situation and requires immediate and large-scale expansion of educational programmes for mature students.

The task is formidable. There are currently only 27,000 places in third-level institutions for mature students and 22,000 of these are for part-time courses. In the age group 25–44, the group most likely to avail of second-chance education, and the group of greatest importance to the country's labour force, there are approximately 650,000 people who have no upper secondary education and 750,000 who have no third-level qualification. Given the size of these numbers, the educational upgrading will have to be gradual, but Ireland must aim ultimately to emulate best international practice in this area, and this will mean that about 25 per cent of all full-time places in higher education should be available for mature students. This translates into about 25,000 places, five times the existing number, and corresponding increases will need to be considered in the number of part-time places.

To achieve such targets a variety of supports and incentives will be needed to encourage potential students to take on the additional work and anxiety and disruption involved in resuming their education. Increased adult educational guidance and counselling must be provided; financial disincentives such as fees must be removed; employers will need to be proactive in providing encouragement and in facilitating the return to education by providing career breaks or flexible working hours as well as financial support where the company will benefit from the educational upgrading.

Universities will need to give a far higher priority to mature student education and to see it as a central part of their educational services. They will have to create special access routes, bridging and orientation programmes to remedy deficiencies in knowledge and to ease the transition back to study, part-time, modularised courses, new modes of delivery, including off-campus provision and the full use of Information and Communications Technology to assist learning and to supplement on-campus teaching with forms of distance education. This will mean departing from cherished methods of pedagogy and devising ways of responding to market needs without discarding the first principles of good education. It will also mean radical changes in the work patterns of staff and extensive training in the new forms of communication. And none of this is likely to

41

happen unless the state shows its commitment and provides assurances that the new services will be adequately financed and will not be a further burden on overstretched budgets and overcrowded facilities.

The other major area of continuing education, postgraduate training to extend the skills of professionals or keep them abreast of developments in their fields, will also involve major adjustments in outlook, systems and work patterns for universities. Course structures, as in the case of mature student education, will need to be flexible, modular and largely part-time. The programmes will, in many cases, have to be delivered outside of regular working hours and the role of computer-assisted learning and of distance education through the Internet will be particularly important.

Universities are best qualified to offer educational services at this advanced level, and Irish universities have shown a ready willingness to assume this responsibility. But they have been impeded by the fact that there is no national policy on professional postgraduate training and no agreement about the providers or the funders. As a result, developments have tended to be haphazard and tentative. This form of education is vital to the knowledge society. Planned development of it must not be delayed.

The problems associated with inequality of educational opportunity are still more urgent and even less tractable. There are whole areas in our cities where up to 60 per cent of young people leave school by age 15 and where only a handful ever reach university. The consequence is continuing poverty, wasted potential, disillusionment and alienation.

The solution will require two principal forms of action.

Attitudes towards education and perceptions that it is useless or unattainable must be changed by counselling, by increasing the resources of local schools, and, most effectively, by involving all age groups in educational activities through a strong system of community education. But all of this must be joined to financial incentives adequate to ensure that young people, for whom release from poverty is the most immediate goal, are not asked to make financial sacrifices to continue their education. The second requirement is the creation of mechanisms to facilitate access for disadvantaged students into third-level.

Universities have a capacity and responsibility to contribute on both fronts. They can have a profound influence on the attitudes and motivation of young people in disadvantaged areas by forming linkages with the local schools with a view to stimulating and supporting higher academic achievement, by encouraging their students to act as mentors to individual primary or second-level students, by using their vast educational resources to expand and strengthen community education.

Universities have a much more direct responsibility in relation to the special modes of entry that will be necessary to accommodate disadvantaged students. They alone can determine entry requirements and assessment procedures for measuring the qualifications of applicants. They should also be centrally involved in the design and delivery of pre-university courses. Most students from seriously disadvantaged backgrounds will need such courses to ensure that they have the knowledge and skills to succeed at third-level. Universities are best qualified to design these programmes, and pre-university courses are best taken in universities where students can become familiar with the university milieu and its approach to learning before they undertake the full burden of degree programmes.

Universities cannot solve the complex social problem of unequal access to education, but they are a key element in its solution, and this needs to be more clearly recognised both by the universities themselves and by all other interests involved.

In conclusion, the emergence of the knowledge age with its profound impact on the educational requirements of developed societies is altering forever the traditional role of the university. The pace and scale of the adaptation required to cope with more diverse student bodies, changing curricula, and new modes of delivery will not be easy to achieve. But the story of the university is one of ongoing adaptation and evolution, and the university will endure so long as it balances its response to particular public needs with adherence to its own basic, independently determined and rationally based educational values.

THE ROLE OF A MODERN UNIVERSITY

Ferdinand von Prondzynski

It is said that when one of Queen Victoria's daughters declared to her mother that she wished to pursue studies in art at a college in London, the queen wrote her a letter in which she warned her, as follows: 'You must beware of College dons, my dear. They mix with all classes of society and are therefore dangerous.' I fear that any lecturers that Princess Louise might have come across would not have been very dangerous. I doubt indeed whether they would have 'mixed with all classes of society'. But if, some 150 years later, we were to set ourselves some goals for the development of our universities, we could do worse than to aim to be intellectually dangerous, or to seek to be more fully part of the social, political and economic structures and networks of the society as a whole. The question I wish to touch on briefly here, therefore, is whether our modern universities would have appeared to Queen Victoria to be adequately frightening, and whether we have a sufficiently challenging vision of our role in society and in public life; and if the answer to these questions is 'no', what we should be doing about it. I may also want to suggest, though only in passing and certainly not *ex cathedra*, how I think my own university, DCU, should position itself in this agenda.

Ferdinand von Prondzynski is President of Dublin City University. Formerly Professor of Law and Dean of the Faculty of Social Sciences, the University of Hull, UK.

Universities exist and must be responsive to the external environment, and this has been undergoing very significant changes over recent years. Some of the more significant developments could be summarised as follows, in no order of priority.

First, the traditional disciplines in the arts, humanities, social sciences and natural sciences can no longer be seen as separate areas of knowledge, study and research. The traditional idea that knowledge is divided into disciplines, and that disciplines are self-contained areas of knowledge with their own exclusive methodologies is no longer easily sustainable.

Secondly, the proportion of the population seeking access to third-level education has risen dramatically. This has been under-pinned by a variety of government initiatives, aimed at bringing a greater proportion of the population into higher education, and aimed also at encouraging 'second chance' access to mature students.

Thirdly, the idea that the quality of what universities do should be assessed independently, with some external controls, has taken root. This is so despite the mixed experiences of quality assurance mechanisms in some countries, in particular in the United Kingdom.

Fourthly, the cost of cutting-edge research, particularly in the natural sciences, has risen dramatically. This has led to a need for universities to seek much larger amounts of funding for research from a wider array of sources, and in turn it has also made the creation of larger research teams, in which economies of scale can be achieved, much more desirable.

Fifthly, an increasing amount of teaching and research is being conducted by independent institutes and business organisations. We have recently seen the gradual rise of the 'corporate' university, and this is a trend that is likely to continue. Furthermore, the emergence of private research institutes doing 'pure' research is also a new development affecting the traditional universities.

Sixthly, economic globalisation has begun to have a direct impact on universities. We have seen the emergence of strong international competition between universities, and a move by some universities (particularly those from the United States of America and Australia) to establish a presence in other countries.

Finally, universities themselves have become increasingly complex organisations, often with significant operational, managerial or financial problems, and an infrastructure not well-equipped to deal with these strategically.

THE SUCCESSFUL UNIVERSITY OF THE FUTURE

Meeting the above challenges will require a re-assessment of whether universities, as they have developed through the centuries in the western scholastic tradition, are correctly positioned to benefit from growing opportunities and to deal with potential threats.

Some values to which universities have traditionally subscribed are, in my view, unchanging. They were perhaps well summed up by John Henry Newman, in his tract *Idea of a University*, as follows: '… A university … has this object and this mission: … its function is intellectual culture; here it may leave its scholars, and it has done its work when it has done as much as this. It educates the intellect to reason well in all matters, to reach out towards truth, and to grasp it'.

47

Perhaps the most dangerous threat universities face is from themselves. Amidst the noble traditions of academic freedom and critical inquiry, there are also some entrenched rigidities that make them vulnerable. In many respects, our universities have developed as cottage industries, even if some of them are delivered out of some fairly venerable cottages. They consist of small units of academic production, working in awareness of new insights and discoveries but as separate individuals or groups. They do not as a whole have a major role in wider policy formulation, nor are they very successful in exploiting their discoveries, either intellectually or commercially. Like many small enterprises, they pay insufficient attention to the qualities of good management that facilitate and support the primary organisational goals. They are aware of, but ultimately do not trust, each other.

It is becoming clear this type of organisational framework will not do any more. The most successful universities (other than a small number of traditional, well-endowed universities) are likely to be those that are able to adopt and successfully implement the following strategic aims:

- they will have a clearly defined and recognisable focus;
- they will place great emphasis on the development and critical analysis of knowledge;
- they will have an understanding of and a place in their strategy for culture and inter-cultural cohesion;
- they will be highly quality conscious;
- they will be organisationally flexible, with speedy and transparent decision-making processes;
- they will place developmental emphasis on areas of study

or research, rather than on traditional disciplines as self-contained units (bearing in mind the words you read on entering the Carnegie Museum in Pittsburgh: 'Knowledge is one. Its division into subjects is a concession to human weakness');

- they will value staff and students and will devolve power and responsibility wherever possible, within an institutional strategic planning framework;
- they will enter into partnerships with each other and with business organisations, government and community groups, often blurring the dividing lines between the university and its partners;
- they will be active participants in global activities and initiatives;
- they will be progressive in the use of new methods and technologies, including in particular the use of new forms of communication;
- they will be commercially successful;
- they will be conscious of their social responsibilities.

It can be argued that universities have been too slow to adopt this agenda for change, and that their standing in society has been weakened as a result. It is my hope for DCU that it will be able to keep in view its original mission of quality and innovation and questioning of received wisdoms in the field of higher education. DCU will aim to be a globally recognised and admired university, generating real excitement and enthusiasm among its various stakeholders.

But this agenda for change is likely to affect all universities in equal measure. Universities are a vital component in any successful economy, but their ability to play a serious role will increasingly depend on their ability to be flexible, non-bureau-cratic and responsive to the changing social and economic needs around them. It may not be an easy objective to fulfil.

THE CHANGING IDEA OF THE
UNIVERSITY

James J. A. Heffron

The past forty years have witnessed extraordinarily rapid and massive change in the universities throughout Europe. Not only have numbers of institutions increased, by two- to three-fold in some countries, but the nature of the activities of the universities has broadened becoming less academic and more vocational in the process. The ancient and old universities have had to face new challenges from other forms of higher education institutions as the transformation from an elite higher education system to mass higher education took place at the beginning of the 1960s. In the Irish university context, we have been strongly influenced by developments in the British university system not only because of its proximity but principally on account of a common language and historical influences. Despite our accession to the European Union in 1973 developments in

Professor James J. A. Heffron is chairman of Convocation of the National University of Ireland. He obtained the PhD degree in Biochemistry from University College Dublin. He has held research and lectureship positions at the Mayo Clinic and Mayo Graduate School of Medicine, Rochester, MN, USA, University College London, University College Dublin and currently at University College Cork. He is a former dean of the Faculty of Science at UCC. He was awarded the Royal Irish Academy Research Medal for distinguished research on the human disease malignant hyperthermia, elected a member of the Royal Irish Academy and awarded the DSc degree for published work on anaesthetic toxicity and muscle disease by the National University of Ireland. He is a former adviser on the toxicity of chemicals in ambient air to the World Health Organisation's European office.

mainland European universities have had little impact here so far. Indeed, it is safe to say that developments in universities in the United States have had a more significant impact on the evolution of the Irish system, *viz.*, the adoption of semesters instead of terms, modularisation instead of subjects, credits rather than whole examinations and even the development of graduate schools. Nevertheless, the university as an institution has survived through eight tumultuous centuries despite numerous European and world wars and profound change in the structure and organisation of society. As remarked by the OECD in *Universities under Scrutiny* (1987) 'economic, social and political organisations have come and gone … yet even the poorest, smallest and newest of the universities of the modern world retain considerable links with their ancient predecessors'.[1]

MEANING OF 'UNIVERSITY'

'University' is a much misunderstood term particularly amongst politicians and the new wave of further education colleges and technological institutes. Many of these institutions aspire to university status on the basis of their importance to the economy, their diversity of courses and often large student numbers. It is a common form of attack of the university sector to label the latter with clichés such as 'ivory towers' and not being in the 'real world'. The universities, on the other hand, are rather passive in their own defence lest they be accused of elitism by the public and the politicians; indeed, the new trend is to continually protest their usefulness to government and to industry and in many instances they hire public relations firms or even set up their own public affairs offices to justify their existence.

Many attempts at defining or explaining the term 'university' have been made. It is appropriate to open this article with a definition again but one which takes into account at least to some degree the evolution of the definition. Historically, the definition which most of us are familiar with is that embodied in Cardinal J. H. Newman's original and famous one set out in his *Idea of a University* (1852).[2] Many will recall that famous essay or discourse of Newman as set out in the *Leaving Certificate Prose* published by the Educational Company of Ireland. Alas, it is no longer on the list of recommended reading for secondary school students. Newman's idea or concept of the university was that it was a community of scholars, teachers and students devoted to teaching and research and in which principles of thought and action are inculcated and expounded. *The Oxford English Dictionary* states that the meaning of the word *university* is the gathering of teachers and students in the pursuit of the higher learning, a definition apparently agreed no less than nine hundred years ago. Another dictionary definition gives the meaning as an educational institution for both instruction and examination in the higher branches of knowledge with the power to grant degrees. The oldest universities had their origins sometime during the twelfth century when they arose from small communities of scholars and teachers that put down roots in such centres as Bologna, Paris, Oxford and Cambridge. These communities evolved by developing curricula, structures and examination systems and were known as *studia generalia* for some time. Originally, the noun *universitas* referred to any privileged corporate body; its restricted meaning of an academic institution involved exclusively in higher learning was apparently not used before the fifteenth century.[3] These early superschools or universities offered a very limited choice of study – theology, arts, law and medicine – compared with the universities of the twenty-first century.

While there is some doubt about the exact time at which the university came to be recognised as such, i.e., as an institution with established location offering higher learning in a number of organised faculties, there is little uncertainty about the role that Newman's *Idea* has played in the development of the university during the past one hundred and fifty years. It provided the blueprint for the emergence of the Catholic University of Ireland despite some clerical opposition. The Irish hierarchy wanted a kind of glorified seminary where young Catholics could be protected from the heretical views of both Trinity College Dublin and the recently founded Queen's Colleges at Belfast, Cork and Galway. The *Idea* – the universal idea – of a university was inextricably linked to the foundation of the Catholic University, a point not much appreciated in Irish universities by either staff or students. The *Idea* has indeed exerted extraordinary influence on the development, discussion and conceptualisation of higher education throughout the western world. At a time when universities, their objectives, curricula, governance and financing have become the focal point of concern and debate at both national and OECD level, even the antagonists would admit to the virtues expounded by Newman. But in Newman's time in the 1860s only a very small section of the population shared in the benefits of a university education and the vast majority was excluded from any higher-level education. In Ireland up to the early 1960s only five per cent of the relevant age group went to university compared with today's figure which

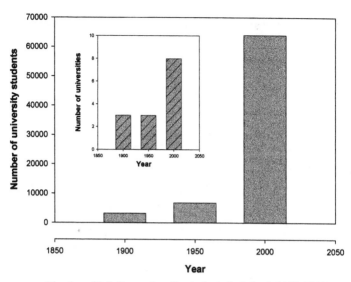

Number of full-time university students in Ireland, 1900–2000
Inset: number of universities in Ireland, 1900–2000

is greater than 40 per cent. Little wonder then that the university was regarded as an elite institution until the massive expansion in student entry that took place in the latter third of the twentieth century *(see above)*. Since 1900 there has been a twenty-fold increase in the number of university students in the Republic of Ireland together with a three-fold increase in the number of institutions with full university status. It is also noteworthy that there are some forty thousand students in the technological institute sector. While this expansion was good and highly desirable on social grounds it was accompanied by declining real resources, increasing university bureaucracy, poor academic morale, declining academic authority and compromised academic standards. Indeed, universities in Britain have been accused by the press of reducing standards and awarding 'dummy degrees'.[4] At a student level, it is patently clear that going to university is no longer the elusive or distinctive target it was in the past. It is now a right and merely another step or passport to a good job. Little attention is given to the appreciative or liberal side of one's selected course or to getting 'a connected view or grasp of things'.

In Ireland, the 1997 Universities Act [5] has already had a further negative effect on the evolution of the university in Ireland with the exception of Trinity College Dublin which succeeded in blocking significant parts of the act through its Private Members Act (2000). The 1997 Act has succeeded in diluting the influence of academics on both the governing bodies and academic councils which are solely responsible for academic standards; it has resulted in diminution of the status of academic staff at all levels and enhanced the roles and caused proliferation of administrators many of whom have had little or no university experience other than as undergraduates, if even that. The lack of empathy of the new types of administration with any idea of the university – together with the passivity of the academic staff – has ensured that Newman's *Idea* is in a moribund state in its country of origin.

THE NEW CENTURY

It has already been remarked that the humanities and liberal education dominated university education in earlier times. But for the past one hundred years, science has played a major role in university faculties and research schools and indeed, contrary to the comments and perception of some commentators on university matters, this at least has been consistent with the *Idea* of Newman. As we enter the new century it is clear that revolutionary developments in science will play an even greater role in the evolution of the university. Governments are more convinced than ever that technological innovation based on major scientific advances such as the Human Genome Project, in computer science and in information and communications technologies, for example, will continue to propel global economic growth. And it is well recognised on both sides of the Atlantic that the university is still the greatest fount of original ideas and thought for making such advances. They may be disappointed, however, for many academics are not convinced that there is a direct relationship between technological innovation and economic growth. Serendipity and cultivation of curiosity, so important in the life of the university, its students and staff, are concepts too diffuse to satisfy the exigencies of governments, their agencies and international corporations.

In many respects the end of the twentieth century has marked a low point for the university. We have witnessed substantial loss of academic freedom particularly in the area of research. Universities are continually being forced to participate in strategic research for governments and the European Union while inadequate state funding has resulted in large multi-national companies effectively directing university research by making large ear-marked grants for applied research programmes and even, in some instances, installing research institutes on university campuses. National and international research funding is directed almost exclusively to large-scale projects or so-called 'big' science usually with an applied direction. Individuals or small groups of academics have been virtually shut out of significant funding so that it is impossible for the thinking academic to test any new ideas of his/her own. Despite assurances of politicians and government, academic freedom – the right to conduct any form of responsible research and new thinking – is gradually being eroded in favour of top-down and politically-directed research. In Europe, this comes in the form of the centralised research programmes of the EU, standardised to the point of total blandness by the Brussels bureaucracy. If one is to survive in the system one has to jump on to some current bandwagon or media-worthy topic usually with the 'stars' who are adept at recognising flashy areas. Serendipity, which has characterised much university research in the past, is being replaced by managed institutional, national and international research programmes. The state purports to support the advancement of learning and increase in knowledge and understanding for their own sake simultaneously with promoting their application for the benefit of society at large. In practice it is becoming clear that the state is only concerned with applications for research backed up with such populist phrases as 'value for money', centres of excellence, etc. Fundamental research, often referred to as 'blue skies' research, is increasingly dependent on philanthropic organisations and wealthy individuals for funding. But such research is the life-blood of the university. It is the enabling process for communicating and developing curiosity in students – the 'how and why' of things and the development of a connected view or grasp of things as well the power of evaluation and of making normative judgements.

THE INTERFACE BETWEEN RESEARCH AND TEACHING
Most universities consider that an effective teaching faculty is critically dependent on a vibrant research environment. Indeed some believe that an institution does not merit the name univer-

sity unless it conducts a significant range of top-class research. But governments, in the light of escalating research costs and a pragmatic research agenda, take the view that not all universities need to conduct research; they are quite content with a university that responds merely to immediate skills demands and that provides a standardised and de-individualised certification programme. The success of the four-year private degree colleges in the United States is usually cited as evidence for this approach. Newman held that university professors and staff should be involved in both teaching and research. I believe that this view is even more valid in the new century. Academic staff and students are floundering in a sea of information, not only in the form of books, journals and official reports but, in the past ten years, with the advent of the Internet, the information burden has become even more acute. We are bombarded every hour at home and at work with e-mails proclaiming the mind-boggling advantages of the latest software package or the omniscience of some new-fangled website. But the modern university student must be able to evaluate and distil this information mountain, sort out the essential from the transient and convert it to knowledge. It is here that the inquiring mind nurtured by inquisitive lecturers and professors can play such an essential role in interpreting the new, albeit much of it apocryphal, information.

CHALLENGES TO THE UNIVERSITY

Universities are deeply conservative organisations and comparatively resistant to change. This is a widely-held public view and much of it is justified. Official circles usually distrust universities not because of any inherent dishonesty or disrespect but rather because of the perceived challenge to authority posed by the nature of the activity of the university. In many respects this is paradoxical given that most universities are involved in producing new information, new insights and knowledge from their research activities. Inevitably, new knowledge will lead to societal change and with it change in the university. Universities appear to be reactive rather than proactive when justifying their existence most often when commenting on the latest round of state funding or research initiatives. They are frequently seen as having a whinging mentality when responding to government initiatives in areas such as disadvantaged student access and life-long learning, for example. Despite this conservatism universities have very tamely allowed increased vocationalism and training functions to enter their long-established faculties and programmes, for example in this country, the proliferation of degrees in nursing, located in the polytechnics in the Netherlands for instance, and many so-called continuing education and technology courses. Many academics view these developments with alarm from the viewpoint of both university function and academic standards. But of far greater significance is the threat of quality assurance and teaching quality assessments. These represent bureaucratic attempts to standardise everything in the university from lecturing to examining, from curriculum design to staff-student discussions, and even from the classical essay to the laboratory experiment. While other levels of education are critical of standardisation and the mass approach to learning, the universities are gearing up with apparent gusto for uniformity and loss of individualisation. In the case of Ireland this is enshrined in the 1997 Universities Act. In Britain they have had the most bureaucratic quality assurance system in Europe for the past ten years and it is clear that we are following in their footsteps. At EU level, a similar standardisation of universities and the courses and degrees offered is envisaged in the 1999 Bologna Declaration. And this despite the success of the inter-European university student mobility programmes, namely, the Erasmus and Socrates schemes. The great attraction of these programmes was the diversity of European university courses in addition to the cultural differences of the host countries. Finally, the impact of the new 'managerialism' introduced under the guise of accountability has reduced the status of the individual academic and even threatens their professionalism and the authority of academic councils.

THE OPPORTUNITIES

The internet and the virtual university are often paraded as challenges to the conventional university. Some would say that they will render the university obsolete. In fact, they can and are being used to complement and reinforce good university principles, aid in study and revision and even reduce pressure on hard-pressed university libraries and their budgets. There are numerous areas where opportunities exist for the university to assert its importance and they arise from many of the universities' recently very prominent scientific achievements to name but a few: the completion of the sequence of the human genetic blueprint, otherwise called the Human Genome Project in February 2001, genetic engineering of agricultural crops and the cloning of human tissues for transplantation. And what about human cloning itself? The university has a unique role in commenting and advising in a dispassionate manner on the ethical issues arising from these important scientific and medical advances and developments. Indeed, it is unlikely that any other human organisation can offer such disinterested and informed comment to the public and to government. But there is one principal impediment lurking: have universities gone too far in accepting capital and research funding from government and industry?

CONCLUSION

The university has shown its resilience and its indispensability as an institution over the past eight centuries. I believe it can do so for the next millennium if it does not sacrifice its intellectual independence merely for earmarked funding, be it from governments or industry. Governments, in particular, owe it to society and to the university to fund the latter in a manner which is fair and allows independence of use – requiring accountability not accounting. Preserving independence of its research and teaching will enable the university to act in line with the *Idea*. Although much has changed in the externals of the university since 1852, the Newmanian goals of achieving a connected view of things and developing the capacity for evaluation and normative judgements are even more necessary in our ever rapidly changing world snowed-under with mountains of information, some important and, no doubt, much trivial.

NOTES

1. OECD, *Universities under scrutiny*. OECD, Paris, 1987.
2. Newman, J. H. (1852), *Idea of a University*, Longman, Green and Company, London.
3. Dunbabin, J. (1999), Universities c.1150–1350', in: *The Idea of a University* (eds. Smith, D., Langslow, A. K.), pp. 30–47. Jessica Kingsley Publishers, London.
4. Smith, A. & Webster, F., (1997) 'Changing ideas of the university', in *The Postmodern University* (eds. Smith, A., & Webster, F.), pp. 1–14. SRHE and Open University Press, Buckingham.
5. *The Universities Act 1997*, Stationary Office, Dublin, 1997, p. 17.

THE ROLE OF THE UNIVERSITY IN THE NEW CENTURY

Miriam Hederman O'Brien

THE DEBATE

Given the nature and range of universities and the manner in which they have become increasingly involved in society over the past 100 years it is not surprising that they have assumed a wide range of roles. Indeed, it would be disturbing if they had not. Neither is it surprising that there is no unanimous agreement about the order of priority of those roles.

Universities have long enjoyed a remarkable degree of independence. They have been granted status and privilege in return for their dual functions of developing the intellectual potential of their students and of providing a resource of knowledge and analytical skills for the community at large. The financial means at their disposal and the source of those funds have varied. As education has become an increasing element of governmental policy, the universities have been brought more into the ambit of the national policy-makers.

It is not clear who are the best arbiters of the elements that constitute the most appropriate and best kind of university

Miriam Hederman O'Brien, BA (University College Dublin); Barrister-at-Law (King's Inns) PhD (Dublin University). Holder of the Killeen Research Fellowship (Dublin University) 1990–1992. Chancellor of the University of Limerick. Vice-President of the European Cultural Foundation. Trustee of the Irish Centre for International Affairs, Louvain. Chairperson of the Commission on Taxation 1980–1985. Chairperson of the Commission on Health Funding 1987–1989.

activity. How important is independence for example and how is it to be defined? For whose benefit should universities function? Where do universities fit in the general framework of national education and scientific research? How should they be funded?

These are major questions. However, I would like to take the opportunity afforded by a publication such as this to focus on some aspects of the relationship between universities and their students in the current environment. That issue is relevant because of the changes that are taking place in the student population and in society in general. University education confers a privilege on those who receive it but our understanding of privilege evolves as our culture changes. Many of my generation were conscious of the sacrifices of others who had enabled us to attend university. There was a certain understanding that we would repay them, in some generally unspecified way, in the future. Most of us expected to emigrate and to contribute to the welfare of our host country. We hoped that we might return to or remain in Ireland – if we were fortunate. We did not normally consider that the university had any particular obligation to us. Circumstances today are quite different but universities, and their students, are still supported by many who cannot attend them.

THE STUDENT AND THE UNIVERSITY

Apart from the students, those affected by the performance and standards of a university include the staff, management, governing authorities, other educational sectors, taxpayers and the wider community, all of whom have stakes in the universities. The students however, constitute the raw material for their work and the achievements of graduates are the ultimate test of their success.

What is a student entitled to expect from his or her university? And what does the university expect of its students?

Having gained 'access', which means achieving a certain level of academic competence at second-level or (for a mature student) proven competence through other means, the university student has to fit into the university framework. For some, this is a logical progression into a discipline for which school has been a preparation. For others, it is a Procrustean nightmare. The university wishing to fulfil its primary role as educator will provide the student with a high level of teaching by experts in the particular fields of the relevant discipline. The matching of student aptitude with areas of study is, however, a more complex issue. Many university teachers would argue that this should have been done in advance and that it is function of the school and the home rather than that of the university. However, the combination of the early age of entry of most Irish students and a haphazard understanding by many people of what different qualifications entail, leaves a sizeable number of confused first-years. Despite the good efforts of many faculties and individual members of staff, students should be warned that, when they reach university, they will not *necessarily* receive the kind of direction they may need.

Undergraduates are entitled to expect a high level of subject-competence in their teachers. The way in which they are taught will be different from their experience at second-level and will require a new approach to learning. It is therefore natural that students attach importance to the teaching and communication capabilities of staff, particularly in first year.

The postgraduate student is most affected by the equilibrium between teaching and research. Any evaluation of third-level education will cover the extent to which the 'teachers' are up-to-date in their chosen field and how they instruct their students in the principles of enquiry and research at the highest level. On the other hand, a researcher, even of international reputation, who cannot communicate his or her knowledge to students should be cherished but largely confined to interacting with his or her peers.

To meet the needs of undergraduates, the art of teaching requires pedagogical skills, and a fair measure of esteem for the process, on the part of members of the university staff. To meet the needs of the postgraduates, the quality of research must be rigorous, in touch with the most up-to-date, internationally accepted developments and relevant to the student's subject.

NEW PATTERNS AFFECTING STUDENT-UNIVERSITY RELATIONS

Recent years have witnessed a great increase in student numbers, improvements in facilities, a change in the competitive atmosphere and, probably, a decrease in the amount of time actually spent on campus.

The multiplication of student numbers naturally puts some strain on the *structure* that has to support them. Even with a recent increase in staffing levels, the ratio of students to staff remains high in Irish universities. 'Talk and chalk' has been superseded by other methods of communicating knowledge but not all members of staff and not all students are ready for the implications of the change. Facilities have improved dramatically. However, despite the new buildings that can be observed on almost every Irish campus, the physical infrastructure is only now coming into line with requirements. Given the speed of developments in science and technology, new equipment will be required on a continuing and regular basis.

Competition begins among applicants and continues as students struggle to sustain or improve their relative position *vis-à-vis* their peers. Irish universities traditionally have had more applicants than places, particularly for the most sought-after courses. This situation is altering gradually. The change in the demographic pattern and the availability of places in universities in other countries will force Irish universities to compete for good students. As the employment market tightens, the flow of postgraduate students, which is so important for the future of a university, may decrease. The competition for graduate students has already, albeit discretely, begun.

The *lifestyle* of students has changed. Fifty years ago, most undergraduates had to live away from home. Financial constraints, lack of private transport and a general acceptance that social as well as academic life revolved around the university, meant that the working week was of at least five and a half-days duration and that college societies and activities provided a wide range of cultural and recreational activities, even on Saturdays. There is now a move to the four-day or four and a half-day week. This is happening in a period when the facilities, as we have already noted, have been greatly improved. Is the university becoming less important in the lives of the students? The pattern of working part-time, at night or during the day, has an effect on the lifestyle of the students involved, which was unknown in an era of high unemployment. The pressures with which students have to come to terms are partially addressed by the support-staff which now operate in universities, either directly or through the students' unions. Most students, however, with the help of their lecturers, colleagues, family and friends have to cope as best they can – just as 'in the old days'.

Students have traditionally challenged received wisdom and custom but such *challenge* was more muted, and limited, when educational authorities wielded a more absolute rule. The relationship between student and university has become more open, more balanced and more mature in recent years. This change has occurred more in some universities than in others and it takes time for an entire institution to adapt to a new approach and a more equable relationship.

Internationalism has become a feature of modern university life, bringing the universities back to their origins as haunts of wandering scholars and research students who wanted to extend their learning as widely as possible. The European Union-wide network of undergraduate interchange has opened a new channel of cultural development for Irish students. Medical schools have had a tradition of students of many nationalities for generations but the inclusion of students from a wide variety of cultures in the humanities and sciences is a welcome addition to the Irish university scene. The reciprocal opportunities for Irish students to take part of their course in another country has also brought a new dimension to the experience and formation of Irish students.

WHAT IS REQUIRED OF THE STUDENT?

There are obvious advantages in competition but it may have unforeseen consequences. The most obvious of these is that the keener the competition the greater the temptation to take what are euphemistically called short-cuts. Facilities for cheating have become more sophisticated and much more numerous. The first requirement for a student is therefore *integrity*.

The process of joint research and mutual learning should begin at the very start of the education process: within the university framework, however, the individual's contribution to the exploration of knowledge is raised to a new plane. This *collaborative* effort takes place in a context in which competition for results has become keener. Despite the tension so engendered, the student has to choose an approach that will also benefit other students/competitors. Knowledge must be regarded as part of an organic process, in which the sum becomes greater as the contributions increase, rather than a cake in which each shared slice decreases the amount available.

University entrance requirements are expected to set a standard to ensure that students are ready to undertake their chosen field of study. In reality, however, the 'points' system is fair but liable to lead to mismatches. If one could make a single plea to students, it might be to seek help to extricate themselves from a field that they have discovered to be the wrong one for them. At the same time, one would have to make a strong plea to the universities to operate a mechanism which would ensure a *reasonable degree of flexibility* in their procedures. In the long run, it is in nobody's interest that a potentially good scientist flounders in law school or that a good historian languishes in business studies.

Modern society supports universities for many reasons but one of the most obvious is based on the assumption that they will produce graduates who will contribute to that society. They will form the administrative, educational, and professional sectors of the community in a manner which will benefit society in general. It is recognised that university education enhances graduates' earning capacity but it is also expected to contribute to the social and economic well-being of the country as a whole.

Because *access* to third-level education is perceived as being of particular benefit to individuals and to the communities in which they live, government policy in many countries, including Ireland, is geared to improving opportunities for students with physical disabilities and those from socially or economically deprived backgrounds to attend university. There is also a policy objective to open up opportunities for older students who were unable to attend university in their earlier years. The universities are therefore expected to devise methods that will support this wide range of students so that they can successfully pursue their studies to the highest standards required. The policy has to be implemented by many bodies and across a wide range of areas in order to make a significant difference but, once the universities have accepted the students, they, as institutions, must be in a position to enable them to achieve their objectives.

The postgraduate programmes of the universities are in the process of expansion. They are expected to meet not only the need for greater depth of research over a wide range of areas but also to train graduates in new areas and subjects, some of which were not in their original disciplines. They can lift acade-

71

mic activity and achievement to a higher and more intensive level. Not only do they provide flexibility for the labour market but also an opportunity for welding new skills and knowledge to the personal and professional experience of their students. Of their nature, they need to be constantly evaluated and, if necessary, re-grouped.

One of the unanswered questions for modern Irish universities is what happens to those *who do not complete* their primary degree courses. Some may take up employment. Others may change course and attend another institution. Others may seem to disappear without trace. But has their experience been of benefit to them? Have they become disheartened by their contact with third-level education? Do they (or their families) consider themselves to have failed? By definition, they are among the intellectually brightest section of the population. Were they ill-prepared, immature, studying inappropriate subjects, subjected to too much of the wrong kind of pressures? To what extent did the factor of addiction to alcohol and/or drugs, which now affects a significant number of young people, cause their departure? How much did university structures contribute to their 'dropout'? If the community expects universities to supply answers to all kinds of scientific, economic and social questions it would be appropriate for the universities jointly to initiate a serious enquiry into this aspect of student life.

Such an enquiry would include a deep and wide consideration of the question of what is the best approach to education. It would involve issues such as the transition from one level of education to another and would build on the research into education already in progress in Ireland. The universities are not entitled to remain indifferent or to consider that the problem of non-completing students is irrelevant to the achievement of their role.

It is accepted that education is increasingly regarded as one of the important factors contributing to economic prosperity and social development. It is common to hear expressions such as 'entrepreneurship', 'innovativeness' and 'leadership' as characteristics that should be fostered within the university system. As with every call for action in the education system, the essential issue lies in the definition. If 'entrepreneurship' is a new title for enterprise, hard work and a positive approach to issues, it is certainly a characteristic, which can be encouraged within the university system. If 'innovativeness' embraces original thought, problem-solving and rigorous research, it is indeed an integral part of university education. If 'leadership' includes a sense of responsibility, an understanding of the dynamics of society and an awareness of what can be accomplished through and for people, it was already included in John Henry Newman's ideal of a university.

The challenge for Irish university staff and students is to make the reality fulfil the hope implied in those expressions.

The Role of the University in
the New Millennium

Tommy Francis

Participation in third-level education in Ireland and throughout the world is higher now than ever before, if measured by numbers of students and proliferation of institutions. The rates of participation of those less wealthy have increased, although it is still disproportionately low. There is in Ireland a perceived shift in the class structure, with the degree of educational attainment being increasingly more important than inherited status in determining material success.

This is all, or perhaps mostly, to the good: yet the growth of the educational establishment has brought paradoxes in its wake. In the primary and secondary schools, the recognition of education as a basic right to be availed of by all has resulted in that right being valued less. Teachers are no longer as respected in their local communities as in previous decades. Third-level degrees are usually required to get a 'good job', but this has changed the status of the degree almost to that of a technical qualification. Where once a leaving certificate was proof of real achievement, now a primary degree may not be enough.

When education is a right (as it should be), it becomes in

Tommy Francis is a graduate of University College Dublin. He teaches English in Pobal Scoil Chloich Cheannfhaola, Co. Donegal and is a former President of The Association of Secondary Teachers, Ireland. He is a member of the Senate of The National University of Ireland and has served on the Council of Convocation.

time routine and taken for granted. The same has happened, for example, with the right to vote. Curiously, the student body of the twenty-first century may have much in common with that of the eighteenth or nineteenth centuries. The majority go to college without having thought about the matter, but simply because it is vaguely expected that they shall, purely because of their family background and social status. At the same time, a small minority have struggled financially to make it there because they think that education has a real value for them.

The twentieth century solved the problems of production, without solving the problem of distribution. There is more than enough food for everyone in a world where many go hungry. There are more than enough material goods in the world, but indeed to become encumbered with material possessions has become a necessity for many in the rich world suffering from luxury fever. Education has perhaps been turned into just another commodity. There is plenty of it being churned out, but is it being distributed properly? Do those who need it do without it? And do those who get it appreciate what they get and use it well?

This of course begs the question of what university education is for.

The twentieth century is perhaps an anomaly in the history of education to speak broadly; educational attainment has become the route to material gain, rather than the luxury good of those who are already at the top of the material ladder.

As a result of this, education has become increasingly a battleground between students. In Ireland, the increasing competitiveness of the secondary education system has bled into the third-level system The course of study culminating in the

Leaving Certificate examinations is perceived, not as an end in itself, but as providing the means to attend university. The course of study culminating in a qualification from a university is perceived as not an end in itself but as providing the means to earn money. And, in an increasingly materialistic and hard-working society (cash rich, time poor), money and the goods it buys are becoming the final end. The security of being in a wealthy society paradoxically discourages risk-taking.[1]

This increased competitiveness has for some decades driven the choices students make about which studies they pursue at university, with people basing their decisions on ultimate material prospects rather than on an intrinsic interest in subjects themselves. Perversely, in some educational systems the greatest competition (and hence the greatest level of academic achievement necessary) is for places on courses that are perhaps less intellectually demanding than others.[2] Demand for opportunities to study higher mathematics is by all accounts less than the demand for media studies, yet one might be judged more intellectually taxing than the other.

If we accept that education being the tool of wealth is an unsatisfactory state of affairs, we can perhaps look at changing it. To look to the new century, we can gain inspiration from the one before last.

The great text of the nineteenth century on education was of course Newman's *The Idea of a University*. Newman's ideal university – and it was an ideal even then – has the end of training good members of society. Whether the nineteenth-century university which informed his thinking came anywhere near attaining that ideal is debatable, but that is irrelevant: Newman gives us ideas which we can translate into our own ideals for a university.

Newman considered attending a university to be primarily a social experience rather than a textual or training one – 'If then a practical end must be assigned to a University Course, I say it is that of training good members of society. Its art is the art of social life and its end is fitness for the world'.

A problem faced by the universities, and society at large, today is that education is increasingly confused with training – that is, narrowly technical training. Driving a car is a useful skill. Imparting training in this skill is important. However the skill is valueless unless one has somewhere of significance to go. Similarly, to have a qualification from a university may enable one to obtain a job, and perhaps indeed to perform that job efficiently. It does not equip one for that portion of life which lies outside earning money, or, as Newman would put it, 'fitness for the world'.

Newman considered the university as having another end beyond the improvement of the individual: it should also improve society as a whole – 'it aims at raising the intellectual tone of society, at cultivating the public mind, at purifying the national taste, at supplying true principles to popular enthusiasm and fixed aims to popular aspiration, at giving enlargement and sobriety to the ideas of the age, at facilitating the exercise of political power, and refining the intercourse of private life'.

These aims are more problematic for today's universities. To put it starkly, these aims are now ideologically suspect. Raising intellectual tone, purifying taste, true principles, refining the intercourse of private life – these raise the ghosts of notions of 'standards', of canons of art, of the dubious notion that there are actually some things that are intrinsically better than other things.

Once self-evident, these notions are now seen as threatening.

To Newman, their self-evidence was obvious. Similarly, he could unembarrassedly use a term like 'man' – there might have been disagreement in his age as to what exactly a gentleman was, but there was no doubt that whatever it was, it was a 'Good Thing'. No university today would dare advertise itself as producing gentlemen, or indeed ladies. Yet at some level one can hope that universities may have some such notion at the back of their minds – what college would dare advertise itself with a slogan like *You will be no better a person after studying here than before you entered*?

But still, the universities cannot successfully resist the pressures of the age. As Newman puts it, 'Wise men have lifted up their voices in vain; and at length, lest their own institutions should be outshone and should disappear in the folly of the hour, they have been obliged, as far as they could with a good conscience, to humour a spirit which they could not withstand, and make temporising concessions at which they could not but inwardly smile'. Ironically, these pressures that may act against their best interests have often originated in the universities themselves. The fiercest attack on canonical literature, for instance, has come from literature departments in universities, not from the mass of people who have not engaged with the canon.

Newman thought that one of the opportunities presented by attending a university – and intellectually, if not morally, the most important one – was that of bringing together young people. 'When a multitude ... come together and freely mix with each other, they are sure to learn from one another even if there be no one to teach them'. This, one hopes, may still be an unintended benefit of a university education, but it is not one that

78

the universities can currently substantially devote their energies to directly facilitating.

Unfortunately, it is easier to point out these problems or fallings short from an ideal than to solve them. The growth and proliferation of the universities and other third-level institutions has made them less uniform (no bad thing), but reduced their ability to act in concert on what might be viewed as an attempt at cultural and social engineering

So, what is to be done? Some of the demographic trends in Ireland may reduce the pressure created by the points system – with the number of 18 year olds in Ireland due to drop by about 30 per cent between 2000 and 2007, the number of people who feel they need to get top grades to enter a university should drop somewhat. If the economic boom continues, many school-leavers will go straight into employment rather than into further education (not, in the long term, a good thing for these school-leavers). These factors might produce a more academically-relaxed student body (albeit a more predominantly middle-class student body).

The idea that education is for life, rather than for youth, should be embraced more strongly by the universities; the resultant changes in the student body could make it fitter for society as it mirrors society more closely.

The universities need to act more strongly in concert: they also need to view themselves as a part of an educational process, rather than fully autonomous.[3] If already existing links with schools are widened and deepened, then all students and their parents could begin to see third-level education as being a natural and integral part of education, rather than an optional extra.

On a final, moral, point, the universities, and indeed the educational system at large, should indeed try to inculcate in its students that their mission is not to make them richer people but to make them better people.

Ireland's universities have a narrow window of opportunity, granted by favourable demographic trends and a booming economy. This opportunity must be seized now if the universities are to have a role in shaping the new millennium, rather than merely existing within it.

NOTES
1: Interestingly, the rapid changes forced upon society by information technology have benefited most strongly (in material terms) those who never attended or dropped out of university. The richest IT billionaires have no degrees apart from those honorary ones granted by universities seeking a share of their wealth. This is not, of course, to suggest that renouncing a university education is a sure-fire road to wealth – for every Bill Gates there are a thousand unemployed and under-educated poor people. Rather, it suggests that a narrow concentration on seeking 'qualifications' is not sufficient for achieving life goals, whatever those goals might be.
2: While the points system is the fairest and most workable option currently available in Ireland, there seems little evidence of a correlation between the high level of points required to enter universities and such things as functional literacy and numeracy.
3: The universities cannot operate in isolation from the other educational institutions, if only because the student body has already undergone most of its formative experiences by the time it leaves secondary school.

THE END OF UNIVERSITY
AUTONOMY IN IRELAND

Seán D. Barrett

June 2000 was intended under the 1997 Universities Act to mark the end of the autonomous university in Ireland. The deadline for the passing by the Oireachtas of a private bill in which Trinity College Dublin and the University of Dublin would petition to end their autonomy passed. The Dáil eventually passed the private bill on 26 October 2000. There was severe criticism of the conduct of the TCD board and college officers in promoting the private bill both within the college and within Leinster House. At the time of writing, it appears that the days of TCD autonomy are numbered. Ireland will then have no autonomous university in the country. The abject surrender of the TCD authorities of the autonomy of that college makes it unlikely that any other Irish university will attain autonomy early in the new century.

As a petitioner against the said legislation in the Oireachtas,

Seán D. Barrett is a senior lecturer in the Department of Economics and Fellow of Trinity College Dublin. He was educated at University College Dublin and at MoMaster University, Hamilton, Ontario. His specialist areas are public policy and transport and he is the author of several books and many journal articles on these topics. He was a director of Bord Fáilte, a member of the Culliton Review of Industrial Policy and of the Review Group on Commercial Harbours. He has been an economic consultant to the European Commission, the OECD, and the European Science Foundation. He is a member of the editorial board of the Journal of Air Transport Management. *He served as Junior Dean and Registrar of Chambers at TCD from 1986 to 2000.*

I believe that universities are not arms of government but communities of scholars. Political interference in universities contradicts the role of the universities as centres of free ideas and expression in a liberal society. Both the civil service and the university have played important roles in the recent evolution of Ireland to a full employment society but their roles are entirely different. Yet, in the 1990s we had a decade of unprecedented legislative, administrative and bureaucratic interference in the scholarly and collegiate functions of our universities. We start the new century at a time when the success of Irish universities has never been greater and morale within them has never been as low.

The attack on Irish university autonomy in the years leading up to the 1997 Universities Act exposed leadership deficiencies in the colleges. A leading business economist said at the time that the defence of university autonomy was weak because 'many university officers already think of themselves as civil servants and saw the legislation merely as a tidying-up exercise. Not for them the challenge of international refereed journals and the free contest of ideas at academic conferences.' The loss of contact with either research or lecturing among the officers of Irish universities seriously weakened universities in their response to the attacks during the mid-1990s from governments and administrators.

Academics relieved of their scholarly duties in order to undertake 'administration' rapidly cease to be academics and become indistinguishable from the administrators, quango members and bureaucrats with whom exclusively they spend their time. An important reform of Irish universities internally is that exemptions from teaching and research should no longer be made when academics become heads of departments, deans or other officers. The goal should instead be that the holders of these posts should remain full members of the academic and scholarly community and in contact with the general student body. The present system has promoted managerialism and bureaucracy, loss of collegiality and undermined autonomy.

The opportunity cost of managerialism and bureaucracy to colleges and their staff is high. Time is the ultimate constraint. Time spent on managerial, bureaucratic and administrative tasks is lost forever from teaching and research in a crowding-out effect. The unfounded criticisms of Irish universities in the mid-1990s might have been better rebutted by university officers more in touch with the basic tasks of the universities.

The result was that the 1990s was a decade of missed opportunities in Irish universities. We chose not to examine the widespread demoralisation of staff in British universities from similar bureaucratic, political and managerial attacks there a decade earlier. Instead of giving all Irish universities the autonomy they deserved we ended the decade with the state's only autonomous university petitioning the Oireachtas to end its autonomy. In contrast to the success of the Irish graduate in academia and employment, our universities stand indicted by external and internal policy-makers on the following grounds; (a) Irish universities are incapable of self-government. Governments should impose board members on universities. (b) Irish universities are incapable of either lecturing or conducting research. Regimes of so-called quality assurance should be imposed by either internal or external bureaucrats. Quangos should evaluate research. (c) Irish academics are unlikely to mark examinations fairly. Regimes of anonymous marking should be imposed.

The response of the officers of Irish universities to these utterly unfounded charges in the mid-1990s was supine. They capitulated on all fronts. The facts are of course that their obsequiousness was utterly unjustified. Irish degrees are in high demand both at home and abroad. Education has transformed the Irish economy and society. Our graduates are in demand in graduate schools worldwide. All this success was attained on a level of funding-per-student of half that in the United Kingdom. The belief in the Universities Act that Irish universities had failed and required the interventions in the act by government to correct for these failures was unfounded. The 'remedies' in the 1997 act should have been rebutted.

Universities petitioning governments to appoint representatives to their boards ignore the experience of board members appointed in this way in other sectors. The system is a form of political patronage and has nothing to recommend it in an era of privatisation. Universities should have led the movement away from political patronage and the brown envelope society rather than be the last to apply to join it. The finance argument in this context is irrelevant. All the available research indicated that the abolition of university fees would have negative educational and social impacts. The increase in the financial dependency of universities on the state does not make a case for state members of university boards. There is no case that by abolishing the private income of a body the state automatically acquires control over its assets as well. It has never been a condition of state intervention in other sectors, that the state acquires the right to nominate board members to the assisted firms or farms.

The irony escaped the university heads that, while they

84

were petitioning governments to become directly involved in running complex and multifaceted universities, the same governments had decided that running a telephone company was too complex a task for the state. The subservience of the university heads contrasted with the successful defence of their autonomy by second-level schools and VEC bodies. We can imagine the response a government seeking to impose its representatives on the boards of private companies or trade unions might receive.

In introducing extra layers of distrust of lecturing staff by university heads extra administrative burdens were added to a low cost university system. This diverts resources away from the primary research and lecturing functions. It also wastes staff time when the alleged goal is to increase the quality of both teaching and research. It is also self-defeating.

Thanks substantially to the success of investment in education Ireland is now a full employment economy. The implications of this for universities have not been properly explored by the university heads. It has become more difficult to recruit lecturers in many subject areas because earnings are so much higher in the private sector. It is unlikely that universities will be able to match the high earnings elsewhere and thus the nonpay aspects of university life may be vital. Setting up mechanisms to waste academic time has seriously eroded the traditional nonpay attractiveness of academe. The repeated votes of no confidence in academic staff by Irish university heads in the 1990s have seriously undermined morale in universities when economic confidence outside the universities has never been higher.

State aid to higher education should be routed through the students. Colleges, which attract students, would thus attract the funds that accompany them. Funding would automatically fall where colleges failed to attract students. Funding based on student preference would not ratchet up further bureaucratic meddling in universities. The colleges might then return to the world of ideas. Like Flann O'Brien's policeman who became mostly bicycle from excessive cycling, Irish university heads have become mostly bureaucrats from man-years in committee. Irish universities and their students will spend the early part of the new century paying dearly for the bicycle-like transformation of university heads in the 1990s.

THE END OF TCD'S AUTONOMY

Had TCD taken a principled stand in favour of its autonomy in the 1990s we might have celebrated 150 years of university education in Belfast, Cork and Galway in 1995 by making all Irish universities autonomous. The TCD case study has negative impacts far beyond the walls of the college.

The hostility of the Education Minister to the independence of TCD caused the then opposition in the Seanad, Fianna Fáil and the PDs, to put down a motion to defend university autonomy for debate on 30 November 1995. It was defeated by 27 votes to 22 with all the university senators voting against the motion.

TCD is a charter corporation. In the High Court decision in *Gray and Cathcart* v. *the Provost, Fellows and Scholars of Trinity College Dublin* in 1910, Mr Justice Ross stated that the state cannot interfere with the charter. It is a contract in perpetuity. Support for that interpretation of charters granted to universities can be drawn from the decision in 1819 of the US Supreme Court in *Trustees of Dartmouth College* v. *Woodward*. The attempt of the State of New Hampshire to alter the charter of Dartmouth College was found to be unconstitutional.

TCD chose not to defend its charter but to enter into confidential discussions with the Department of Education. Walshe maintains 'that the consultation process with the university heads did, however, allow for a large measure of agreement to be reached on the issue of the governing structures.'

The confidential discussions resulted in the body corporate of TCD, some 258 people comprising the Provost, Fellows and Scholars, having no input in framing the legislation that was to be lodged in Leinster House in their name. The body corporate met only after the bill was lodged and then only by order of the College Visitors, the Chancellor of the University of Dublin, Dr Frank O'Reilly and Mr Justice Henry Barron of the Supreme Court. The confidential negotiations also weakened the autonomy of TCD by treating it as a matter of arithmetic rather than one of principle.

The private bill contained elements such as ministerial and outside board representation, regional education boards, changes in the body corporate and the power to abolish the TCD board which had been voted down by the Fellows, the major group in the body corporate purporting to promote the bill at the Oireachtas.

Early in 2000, it became apparent that the University of Dublin, despite appearing in the title of the Private Bill, and being cited in the preamble as a promoter of the bill, had not been consulted. The bill had to be extensively amended to exclude references to the university. Other amendments included errors in Latin translation. The Senate of the University of Dublin is a body corporate comprising the Chancellor, Dr Mary Robinson, Doctors and Masters of the University. In a letter dated 23 October 1996 the Registrar of TCD refused a request that the Senate should discuss the public and private legislation on university governance then proposed. The exclusion of the references to the University of Dublin from the TCD Private Bill does not in my opinion extricate the TCD Private Bill from the requirement to consult the Senate of the University of Dublin. In both the 1873 and 1907 legislative threats to the TCD charter the Senate of the University of Dublin was allowed to debate the issue. The meetings were presided over by eminent legal Vice Chancellors, respectively, Charles Napier and Digby Madden. The requirement to consult the Senate of the University of Dublin in regard to changes in the charter of TCD is also stipulated in the Government of Ireland Act, 1920.

The expiry day for the TCD Private Bill was 16 June 2000, three years after the coming into effect of the 1997 Universities Act. The promoters were allowed an extra 130 days to have their private bill passed by both Houses of the Oireachtas. The extra time given to the promoters was another obstacle placed in the way of those who petitioned and voted against the bill. The use of shameful methods to attain a shameful goal must be an ominous sign. I hope, against experience, that it does not set the precedent for the role of the university in the new century.

REFERENCE
Walshe, J., *A New Partnership in Education*, Institute of Public Administration, Dublin, 1999.

THREE SPRINGBOARDS TOWARD RADICAL CHANGE?

Feargal Quinn

Down through the centuries, universities have shown themselves to be pretty good at adapting to wide changes in social and economic conditions, and at emerging from the adaptation in a form that was not fundamentally different. Can this kind of transformation continue into the third millennium? Or will the forces of change be strong enough to force the creation of an entirely new university model?

I do not have the answer, but I venture to suggest that at least three forces are at work that might be springboards for change that would be radical rather than evolutionary. These forces are:

- the trend towards universal access to universities;
- the trend towards life-long education;
- technological changes in the way we access and disseminate information.

Let us look briefly at each of these factors in turn.

Feargal Quinn is the Dublin-born founder of Superquinn, a supermarket group with a worldwide reputation for innovation and customer service. A commerce graduate from UCD, he has been an independent Senator in the NUI constituency since 1993.

For most of the time that universities have existed, their 'cus-tomers' – that is, their students – have been drawn, almost ex-clusively, from a narrow social elite. I cannot believe that the third millennium will be going very long before this favourit-ism is replaced by universal access to a university education, irrespective of the social or economic background of the stu-dent.

In fact, I have to pinch myself when I read the sober reports detailing that such discrimination still exists at all. If we were talking about feudal times, or even the early days of the indus-trial revolution, I would not find it hard to believe: it could be seen as all very much of a piece with societies that condoned slavery or denied votes to women. But in today's day and age? Especially since it is an era where universities (in Ireland, at any rate) are almost exclusively funded by the general taxpayer?

To draw attention to the fact that universities are still, over-whelmingly, restricted in their intake to the better-off is not to take aim at the universities themselves. They have, by and large, done as much as reasonably could be expected of them to widen access across the social spectrum. But the fact is that these ini-tiatives have been unsuccessful: recent research shows that vir-tually no progress has been made over the past 20 years. That failure is not the fault of the universities: it is due to a failure to address the problem of disadvantage throughout the education system. A significant proportion of our children enter the edu-cation system disadvantaged, and many of them become more disadvantaged the longer they remain within it.

The culmination of this is that fully one-fifth of the age cohort does not finish secondary education at all, and that one-fifth is determined not by innate ability but by social and economic conditions. With that as prologue, the discrimination in university intake is inevitable.

But taking the longer-term view that a millennium perspective allows, I am optimistic that our society will not tolerate this situation for very much longer. The fact that we have failed to make much progress with the problem so far will, I hope, encourage us to look for new ways rather than to abandon the goal altogether. I believe that sooner rather than later, we will see the kind of socially-balanced intake to our universities that we would expect of a democratic republic with our historical background.

What are the implications of such a change for the universities themselves?

They will have to move from the situation of serving only a part of the public to one where they must serve everybody. The courses they offer, and the way they teach them and assess them, will need to be suitable for everyone. No longer will they be able to define an elite in terms that are comfortably class-bound; no longer will they be able to judge performance along a single parameter of intelligence.

How to achieve this, without falling into the opposite trap of 'dumbing down'? How, in particular, to maintain in an era of universal access the university's other great role – to push out the frontiers of knowledge?

These are questions to which I do not know the answers, but I can readily see that they will pose a challenge to the continuance of the university model as we know it today.

Even more challenging is the increasing irrelevance of the time-frame on which university education has traditionally been provided.

Since universities first came into being, their teaching role was seen as one that was focused exclusively on young people. You left school and went to college, which equipped you for a lifetime career. Unless you were cut out to be an academic, the university usually ceased to play any further role in your life beyond your early or middle 20s.

The increasing number of mature students, a recent feature of university life, doesn't really threaten that model: they are seen, and for the most part treated, as people who are simply going through their post-school phase a little later than most.

But what does threaten the model is the revolution that took place in twentieth-century knowledge and blew apart the assumption underpinning the post-school model: the assumption that there is a body of knowledge that changes so slowly one dose of it is good enough to last you a lifetime.

In the new world of knowledge, everything changes all the time – and the idea of stocking people up with enough know-how to last a lifetime has become laughable.

But we have not yet changed our institutions to reflect this new reality: universities still see their main teaching job as the education of undergraduates who come to them straight out of school. The balance of the university's gravity is still heavily on that phase of education, with later initiatives being seen as merely 'top-up' additions. To continue to organise universities in this way is surely to miss the whole point of what lifetime learning is all about.

What kind of university would we have if a university education came to be seen not as a one-off, up-front affair but as something that took place in instalments – spaced throughout one's adult life? What if the first period you spent at a university confined itself to no more than a grounding in the principles – principles that would be built on by successive phases of life experience and further learning?

I remember once challenging a university president with this vision, and asking: could the universities adapt to such a radical change? It is one thing to have a student body that consists primarily of young people, with just a sprinkling of mature students. It is quite another to envisage an institution in which the bulk of those learning, at any one time, would be older people who had already made their way in the world. Wouldn't this require a wholesale shake-up in teaching techniques, a complete recreation of the concept of 'student culture'?

His answer surprised me. He said, with impressive confidence, that changing the universities would be no problem at all. But changing the Department of Education would be the real issue, because the entire framework of the state's financial support for universities is based on the output of undergraduates. To change the universities, you need to change the way they are funded!

I prefer to give that response an optimist's spin, and treat it as making the problem easier rather than harder. If the issue is a political one, then I believe it can be solved in time – because eventually politics tends to bow to reality.

Of the three springboards towards radical change I have sing-
led out, I see as by far the most powerful the new ways we have
developed to access and disseminate information.

This has happened side by side with the explosion of knowledge itself: so not alone do we have an exponentially increased
body of knowledge to cope with, we also have a totally new
framework for storing that knowledge and passing it on.

Traditionally a university had to be a single entity in a particular place, because only then could you bring together the
people with knowledge and the books that contained the knowledge. Taken together, the learned people and their books became a repository of knowledge. The students got their knowledge from the learned people through lectures and from the
books in the library.

That was then. But now, the revolution in telecommunica-
tions and information technology has destroyed that fundamental rationale for a bricks-and-mortar university:

- Learned people can make themselves available to students far more efficiently through electronic means.
  Lectures can be done only once and recorded, freeing
  up the teachers for personal interaction with individual
  students – electronic interaction, of course.
- Students' home computers give faster and more comprehensive access to information than any university
  library, however well-endowed. Not only do the students not have to fight for space in the library, they
  don't even have to travel to it.
- The collaboration between students, socialising and net-

94

working, that is so important a part of university life could be equally well-founded on an electronic model. Indeed, if it becomes any more difficult to travel physically around our big cities, the electronic basis may be much more practical!

University campuses are often impressive, sometimes beautiful and always expensive. But I wonder if we were inventing the concept of a university today, would we base it on the campus model?

Could it be that the very walls of academe have passed their sell-by date, and should now be replaced by an entirely new and more cost-effective approach?

HAVE INTELLECTUALS FAILED IRELAND?

Brendan Ryan

In *Tableau III* 'Arguments', John Murphy argues eloquently that educational values are the necessary bedrock of a proper third-level education.[1] In the same vein considerable thought and paper has been devoted to the need to ensure that engineers, when they arrive in the world of work, possess not just technical skills but the ability to think, to work collaboratively and to understand the social context within which they work.

Yet, from the non-specialist perspective, and in particular the perspective of a practitioner of politics, capacity for serious creative thinking seems largely absent. This absence in turn limits the vision of politicians who are by and large more popularisers than originators of new ideas. Most of us read extensively even if perhaps not deeply enough. We are, all of us, confronted by the problems of Irish society and it is from us that responses are required. And since it seems to me, at least, that problems are almost by definition always new, responses must usually be new as well.

Brendan Ryan is a representative of NUI graduates in Seanad Éireann. He was a senator first from 1981 to 1993 and was re-elected in 1997. He is a graduate of UCD with a degree in Chemical Engineering and lectures in that subject in Cork Institute of Technology, where he has been involved in research related to cleaner production and clean technology. He is also Honorary President of Cork Simon Community and has been involved in campaigning on behalf of homeless people since 1975. He has written extensively on political and other issues and is the author of a book on Freedom of Information in Ireland.

It is in that context that I would judge the general Irish intellectual discourse to have been substantially a failure over the past number of years (or at least the twenty or so years since I first became involved in national politics).

Three areas come to mind. The first is the area of economic policy, the second Northern Ireland and the third the area of church-state relations. To me it seems the evidence is over-whelming that major progress in each area has been made in spite, not because, of the activities of the Irish intellectual class whether based in academia, the media, or the world of letters. Space does not permit me to deal at length with all three so I will concentrate on the matter of political economy. On the other two topics, it is sufficient for the sake of illustration to point out that much of 'intellectual' Ireland is still struggling to come to terms with the reality of a permanent ceasefire, with the accep-tance of the principal of consent and with the changes that are painstakingly emerging. In the intellectual discourse of the pre-vious thirty years the sort of political process and the under-lying analysis that went with it which brought us to where we are were largely dismissed in favour of a one-dimensional and one-sided analysis. That analysis overwhelmingly focused on the failures of Irish nationalism, and the need for us to accept the reality of Northern Ireland. The complexity of living in Northern Ireland and the need for the minority in Northern Ireland to be dealt with according to the same principles that applied to the minority on the island of Ireland was not a part of this analysis. Hence, the shock when first of all a permanent ceasefire and then huge political progress happened.

Sloppy analysis led to sloppy partial conclusions and left us waiting perhaps ten years longer than was necessary for the beginnings of peace.

Peace is of course linked with the religious divide on this island. The consequences of that divide and the limited and often self-serving responses of the churches to it are visible to all of us. But intellectual discourse has managed yet again to simplify all that, and in the process distort reality almost beyond recognition. Again, this deserves greater elaboration, but one simple example might provoke some thought. It is a matter of fact, as far as much of intellectual Ireland is concerned, that Irish sexual mores were so profoundly puritanical because of the dominance of the Roman Catholic Church. The inconvenient evidence that such sexual puritanism is hardly visible in all the other countries where Roman Catholicism is dominant is ignored. (Criminal sanctions against homosexuals were never a part of the law in many southern European countries for instance). A far more plausible explanation for Ireland's historically brief flirtation with puritanism seems to me to relate to our links with Britain and in particular Victorian Britain.

Both of these topics are interesting but they are, to a degree, part of our past. Economic policy, its purpose and content, is far more current and topical. Much of what is written on this topic, in the name of analysis is also unfortunately hopelessly deficient and uselessly derivative. This is particularly true of economics as it is presented through and by the media.

The limited data-set out of which popularising economists draw their information has always been a matter of amazement to me. This first impinged on me when I entered politics and has sadly been confirmed by twenty years of experience! During the 1980s, 'competitiveness' was, it seems to me, invented as a concept in political economy. Competitiveness was the concern which motivated demands for real wage reductions, for cut-backs in public expenditure and for an indefinite delay in the provision of even the most rudimentary provisions of a welfare state. It came as a shock then to discover that in an era when Ireland was, we were told, losing competitiveness, we had in fact a more rapid growth in industrial exports than virtually every country in the OECD! Many enquiries failed to elucidate any convincing explanation as to why a country that was deemed to be losing competitiveness could have a booming export section! Equally disconcerting was the abiding emphasis on lowering taxes as a necessary condition for economic growth. It was obvious again from OECD figures that countries with differing levels of tax 'burdens' had levels of economic growth that correlated not at all with their levels of taxation. This was equally true for unemployment. Extensive enquiries yet again failed to attract convincing or indeed even plausible explanations. Inconvenient data it seemed was best omitted.

Nothing much has changed in recent times. There has been considerable emphasis on deregulation in recent years, particularly on deregulation of the labour market. One manifestation is the insistence that mandatory trade union recognition would deter Foreign Direct Investment. And in the context of globalisation that, it is clear, would be close to disastrous. Another is the consensus that extremely low corporate taxation is central to our drive to attract a continuing flow of such investment. And, of course, the centrality of ever decreasing personal taxation in all of this is rarely challenged either. Any challenges that do arise relate almost exclusively to fears about inflation.

It is intriguing even to list facts that rarely enter public discourse. A highly regulated country like the Netherlands has a lower unemployment rate than the US. A country like Finland can propose a level of paid paternity leave which we would be told was suicidal. Perhaps the most telling fact however is the reality of Foreign Direct Investment. Isn't it a little strange that the fact that Sweden is proportionately more successful at attracting Foreign Direct Investment than any other OECD country rarely enters our argument on political economy and related issues? Much of what we are told is certainty in economics is called into question by that fact alone. If a country where taxation represents well in excess of 50 per cent of GDP, where almost 90 per cent of the work force is unionised, where workers' rights to participation are solidly established, and where welfare is generous can attract FDI on an unprecedented scale then much of what we have been told about the disincentive effect of regulation, taxation and welfare is open to question. Nor of course is the continuing success of the Nordic welfare state model allowed to give the lie to the certainties of Irish intellectual discourse. To the external observer, or the politician anxious to learn from the intellectual endeavours of others, the suspicion that facts are left out if they confuse an otherwise simplistic argument makes such intellectual endeavour entirely worthless.

For the process of political debate this leaves us at a considerable disadvantage, and indeed could have been disastrous in the past. Some feel it may well lead to disaster in the future. If we had, for instance, paid too much attention to the more vocal and visible among our academic and media economists, we would have cut back dramatically on investment in education, and in particular in third-level education. This was a constant repetitive mantra of the 1980s, expressed in two easily popularised slogans. The first was the assertion that it was pointless to educate vast numbers of young people simply to allow them to go and add to the strength of the US/UK economies. We were, it was asserted, simply subsidising those economies. The other slogan was subtler, appealing to an innate sense of justice. It said that subsidising third-level education was a further subsidy to the already well-off. And in a country with almost third-world conditions in primary schools, this assertion had a certain resonance.

Fortunately not too much heed was paid to these demands and the highly skilled products of the 1980s are perhaps the single greatest reason why our economy has finally begun to perform. Some people never learn though. The Department of Finance still insists on describing expenditure on education as 'social' (and by implication non-productive) expenditure!

Two fundamental errors lie behind our selectivity, confusion and apparent determination to avoid or omit inconvenient information. The first is confusion between economic growth and economic development. This confusion arises because most economists still believe that not only is the market the most efficient mechanism to generate resources, but it is also the most efficient method to distribute those resources. Countries like Sweden, Denmark, the Netherlands and others quite clearly think differently. They use the market effectively to create wealth, and then use the wealth, via the state and various redistributive mechanisms to promote development, which they recognise is not synonymous with growth.

The second error is more fundamental. It relates to the way in which we as a society approach all our problems. It relates too to our approach to education and to those educational values cited by John Murphy in *Tableau III*. If our society is to be imaginative and creative in dealing with both the problems of success and the persistent social problems that bedevil us, then our approach must not be guided by either ideology or selectivity. We must, as all students should learn, first of all define the real problem, and then examine all possible solutions. Following that can come the choice of solution, implementation and evaluation.

Our tragedy up to now is that either ideology or laziness has driven us to incorrectly define problems (whether it be in relation to the economy or Northern Ireland). This is compounded by the deliberate omission of working solutions apparently because they are radically different or ideologically unacceptable. (I find it impossible to accept that Irish economists for instance are unaware of the success of the Nordic countries!)

Such an approach, in which all options are explored, and evaluated dispassionately represents the true role of the intellectual in society. It is the role of politics to respond to those ideas, inevitably selectively, and perhaps sometimes dishonestly! As we stand, the situation seems quite different. It is the intellectuals who are selective and the politicians who have had increasingly to ignore them. This makes for limited politics, poor public discourse and ultimately perhaps disaster.

REFERENCE

1: *Tableau III*, Cork Institute of Technology, 2000

THE BIRTH OF THE SPACE AGE ABROAD AND AT HOME

Susan M. P. McKenna-Lawlor

When people in future times look back to the achievements of their ancestors, the twentieth century will be for ever celebrated as the one in which, for the first time, man found the technological means to escape the bonds of gravity and enter the realms of space.

To do this has been to realise an age-old dream, as attested by the fact that fictional flights from the earth have been described throughout world literature. For example, the Greek satirist Lucian (*circa* AD. 190) had one of his characters don vulture and eagle wings and fly from Mt Olympus to the moon in an effort to determine how the stars came to be 'scattered up and down the heavens carelessly'. Over one hundred fictional descriptions of lunar voyages (including works by Cyrano de Bergerac and Daniel Defoe) were published in Europe between 1493 and 1783 following which, the stimulus of the first balloon ascents set the French artist Gustave Dore to illustrate, through the medium of a famous painting he devised in the late 1800s, his

Professor Susan M. P. McKenna-Lawlor is a graduate of University College Dublin and a member of the Senate of NUI. She has been responsible for many pioneering experiments, flown on space missions launched by the four major space agencies and has published more than a 100 scholarly papers in this regard. She is the recipient of a number of international awards including Honorary Citizen of San Jose, USA (for technological achievement); The Russian Tsiokovsky Gold Medal (for Outstanding Contributions to Cosmonautics) and The Irish Laureate Woman of Europe Award. She is presently a guest professor of the Chinese Academy of Sciences.

vision of how a 'Voyage to the Moon' might be implemented.

In a more concrete approach, Isaac Newton in his *Principia* (1687) published a diagram of a ball fired from a cannon located on a mountaintop, with the barrel shown pointing parallel to the ground. In an accompanying 'thought experiment', made in the light of his First Law of Motion (namely that 'a body remains stationary or moves in a straight line unless a force acts on it'), coupled with his theory of how gravitational attraction would be exerted by the earth on the cannon ball, Newton described two key situations. In the fist, he noted that, if the launch speed of the cannon-ball were too low, the force of gravity would pull it back towards the earth and it would resultingly fall near the cannon, having described a curved trajectory. At a higher (critical) speed however (estimated to be 8 kms just above the atmosphere), although the trajectory of the cannon-ball would again curve towards the ground, the surface of the earth, being round, would itself curve away at the same rate and the projectile would resultingly travel all the way around the earth in a circular orbit. Thus, in the seventeenth century, the launching of a satellite into earth orbit could already, at a basic level, be conceptualised and from thence it was but a further small step to estimate the escape velocity (11 kms just above the atmosphere) that would allow a body to be propelled away from the earth, never to return.

Although cannons are impracticable as a means to allow bodies to achieve escape, or even circular, velocity, the advanced development of rockets, implemented by such pioneers as the Russian Konstantin Tsiolkovsky (*circa* 1898) and the American Robert Goddard (in the 1920s), quickly provided the next link in that chain of development leading to the realisation of space-travel. In particular in this regard, at the end of the Second World War, a team of over one hundred German rocket experts lead by Werner von Braun moved from Germany (where they had worked on the V–2 guided missile), to the United States, thereby providing the technology transfer that allowed President Eisenhower to announce by 1955 that the United States would launch a satellite during the International Geophysical Year (1957– 1958).

In the event, to the consternation of the American establishment, it was to be the Soviet Union that actually launched the world's first artificial satellite on 4 October 1957. This was an 83–kg instrumented laboratory called *Sputnik I* followed, in November of the same year, by the half-ton *Sputnik II* that, famously, carried a dog on board as a passenger. The more modest first American satellite *Explorer I* was orbited on 3 January 1958 and, as the American programme thereafter advanced in strength and achievement, the Soviet Union attained, in parallel, a series of remarkable firsts, including being the first nation to mount an unmanned photographic mission to the moon (*Luna 3* on 6 October 1959), and the first to orbit a man around the earth (Yuri Gagarin on 12 April 1961).

Against this background of Soviet achievements, the political desirability of developing relevant technology to a level that would allow an American to plant an American flag on the lunar surface 'before the end of the decade' (not to say before a global television audience), stimulated politicians and businessmen in the United States to support this goal with all of the resources necessary to achieve it. In consequence, backed by a financial injection of some $20 billion, the practical effort required to overcome the earth's gravity, while also controlling those complex circumstances which could lead, within the required time frame, to a safe return mission to the moon, was urgently mounted at NASA. The strategy developed involved sending a three-man crew, one to navigate an orbiter and two to descend to the lunar surface aboard a module that could, in the post-exploration phase, be re-launched to return to the mother ship. Using this philosophy, two American astronauts successfully descended to the lunar surface from the spacecraft *Apollo 11* on 20 July 1969, and transmitted from thence to the world news of the fulfilment of the ancient dream of mankind to reach the moon in their famous message 'The eagle has landed'.

In the years that have intervened since those heady days, spacecraft have already been sent, some with unmanned landers, to all the planets of the solar system except Pluto. Also, several missions have specialised in making *in-situ* studies of comets, because these objects importantly retain in their make-up the primitive material from which the solar system initially formed. Yet, other missions have monitored the dynamic activity of our nearest star, the sun, and monitored the influence of its electromagnetic and particle emissions on the earth. Further, spacecraft in orbit above the earth's atmosphere have viewed the sky across a wide range of wavelengths, thereby detecting the shape of our galaxy, while studies of a weak radiation field pervading space are interpreted to provide insights into circumstances attending the birth of the universe in *The Big Bang*.

To date, twelve American astronauts have landed on the surface of the moon where, in addition to conducting a large number of scientific studies, they collected from six different sites a total of more than 380 kg of lunar rocks for subsequent study on earth. In addition, since its launch in 1986, astronauts from many nations have lived and worked for long periods aboard Russia's large orbiting space station *Mir*. Also, from close to the end of the year 2000, the international space station has provided in low earth orbit (in an environment of near-zero gravity and near-perfect vacuum), a manned research centre for scientific studies, as well as for the development of new commercial products and industries. Relative to this astronaut-related activity, which can be expected to ultimately lead to colonisation of the moon and of the planet Mars, in-depth studies of space biology and of related medicine are now urgently required in order to adequately understand (and where necessary combat), the biological consequences for our species of living and working for prolonged periods in an extra-terrestrial environment.

IRISH INPUTS

In looking back now, as requested by the editors, over my own professional career in space physics, I can note that, by coincidence, this began on the very day *Sputnik I* was launched (on that auspicious day I initially went to the astronomical department of the Dublin Institute for Advanced Studies at Dunsink Observatory as a scholarship student and became the first person in Ireland to report to the press on the passage above our island of this historic spacecraft). Thereafter, I have been greatly privileged to have participated in some of those missions marking the early development of space exploration and have thereby experienced at first hand the excitement and challenge of learning to obtain scientific data across a 'new frontier'.

The first missions in which I was involved in the United States, namely the manned *Skylab* mission which made seminal observations of the sun and its follow up the unmanned *Solar Maximum* mission which was designed to study in depth dynamic solar activity, constituted for me the raising of a curtain yielding insights into solar processes that were, until that time, undreamed of. Thereafter, when I returned to Ireland to take up a position at what was then St Patrick's College (now the National University of Ireland at Maynooth), this and related background experience enabled me to assume leadership of a team that proposed and constructed the first Irish scientific experiment accepted for flight on a European Space Agency (ESA) mission, namely the historic *Giotto* mission to comet Halley. The experiment concerned I called EPONA, a name that, while it provides an acronym for Energetic Particle Onset Admonitor and thus conveys the function of the instrument, also constitutes the name of a Celtic Goddess associated with the commencement of the solar year – thereby linking Ireland's ancient past with the frontiers of space exploration.

The signal scientific success of EPONA during the Halley mission (encounter March 1986) was followed over the next six years by the acquisition of further pioneering data during *Giotto*'s historic earth flyby in 1990, and again during its transition of comet Grigg-Skjellerup in 1992 – in the close environment of which latter object a signature suggestive of the presence of a companion comet was identified in the EPONA particle data. Meanwhile, in the aftermath of the success of 1986, an invitation to fly a further Irish energetic particle experiment at 'The Red Planet' during Russia's *Phobos* mission to mars and its moons was received and accepted. The *Phobos* mission was launched in July 1988 from the Baikonur Cosmodrome and, during planet encounter, pioneering data secured by the Irish instrument (which was called Sled), lead to the identification of various populations of high energy particles in the close planetary environment – observations that are currently of particular interest in relation to the planning of future manned missions to this planet.

Over the succeeding years, Irish experiments have already been flown, or are currently in preparation for being flown, by my group on missions launched by the five major space agencies (European, Russian, American, Japanese and Chinese). For example, the Irish national instrument Lion which was designed and built at Maynooth and flown on ESA's Solar Heliospheric Observatory (SOHO), has monitored, since soon after its launch in 1995, solar particle emissions from a position in space which allows observations of the sun to be made continuously. The data obtained at this location (called the L 1 Lagrangian Point) are not only important in monitoring space weather, but are also expected to contribute downstream towards revealing the influence of solar activity on data measured aboard four spacecraft of ESA's *Cluster* mission – which were very recently launched to operate compositely as a constellation monitoring a range of phenomena in the close earth environment. It is of Irish interest that *Cluster* carries aboard each of its spacecraft an instrument named Rapid which was partly designed by my group, and is specially configured to monitor dynamically changing supra-thermal plasma distributions in those separated regions of geospace through which the individual *Cluster* spacecraft fly.

Complementary data secured by a further rapid instrument flown aboard the Japanese mission *Geotail*, as well as by a differently configured plasma instrument named Waves, to which my group also contributed design/construction expertise for

NASA's space mission *Wind*, are presently poised, pending the commissioning of the four *Cluster* spacecraft, to input to a multi-national investigation of fine details of the complex interaction between the solar wind and the near earth environment, with particular emphasis on determining how mass, momentum and energy are transferred around the earth at different places and at different times. A neutral atom spectrometer called Nuadu, currently under construction for China's *Double Star* mission, is designed to later contribute yet further to these investigations from a polar orbit around the earth.

Space research in the realm of fundamental physics will shortly be implemented by NASA's flagship *Gravity Probe B* mission (*GPB*) which is designed to test two important predictions of Albert Einstein's general theory of relativity – namely that space and time are warped by the presence of the earth and that the earth's rotation drags space time around with it. The delicate measurements required to detect these effects can be disturbed by electrical charging and heating effects produced by ambient high-energy particles in the medium through which this spacecraft will fly. Monitoring and taking account of the influence of these high-energy particles on *GPB* is therefore essential to the successful realisation of the precise measurements required to test Einstein's theory. In this connection, an innovative, highly sophisticated, particle monitor has been designed and constructed for this spacecraft by my group that has advanced capability to detect the particle radiation concerned while remaining resistant to its deleterious effects.

A further exciting mission currently under development, this time in Europe, is *Rosetta* which, among other objectives, is scheduled to land an unmanned spacecraft on the surface of the nucleus of comet Wirtanen. Material drilled from beneath the surface of the cometary nucleus will be analysed by the on-board *Cosac* experiment (in which I participate) in an effort to identify organic molecules that constitute the pre-biotic building blocks of life. A search will also be made using this sample for incorporated material pre-dating the formation of the solar system.

Other experiments currently under construction include an instrument (Aspera-3), developed in association with a group from Sweden, that will investigate during ESA's *Mars Express* mission the interaction of the solar wind with planet Mars and seek to determine what it was that caused Mars to change from being a warm and wet planet to its present status of a cold and dry one. A further instrument (Sir) designed in association with a group from Germany, will study the characteristics of lunar rocks during ESA's forthcoming *Smart* mission, with a view to gaining new insights into the origin and early history of the moon.

A personal experience of immense excitement and pleasure during the present year was that of floating in micro-gravity for a total of six minutes. In the glorious sensation of, thereby, being 'able to fly' it seemed, as never before, that I was an integral part of the movement that is presently carrying mankind towards a new destiny in space, and it thus seemed an entirely suitable way for a space scientist to greet the dawning of a new millennium!

In the last century universities, through university scientists such as myself, have, across the world, played an integral role in the planning and implementation of early space exploration. In this connection, suitably competent academics were consistently invited to serve on study teams and on key internal and external advisory committees within the major space agencies and have, thereby, been involved in laying out long-range goals, objectives, strategies and priorities for the implementation of space missions. Further, university scientists have served as principal investigators for the development of mission investigations and, associatively, pioneered new approaches to measurement making – thereafter also carrying out within their groups the long-term laboratory theoretical and computational studies required to fully interpret and understand the data returned from individual space science missions.

In the new century, contributions to discovery and synthesis, to new ideas and to innovative technologies will again comprise the key activities of university-based space scientists, while those at the leading edge will, in addition, contribute to the formation of that steady stream of highly-trained and motivated graduates required to assure a viable future for the discipline of space research.

Meanwhile, the changing character of space science missions from major, long lead time, odysseys to small, frequent and relatively low cost missions which demand extensive enabling technologies, is already allowing some universities to take on responsibility for the design, development and operation of entire spacecraft. Further, the trend towards providing easy electronic access to archival space data, together with new policies to place such data very quickly in the public domain, increasingly allows postgraduate students to participate, under academic supervision, in the analysis and interpretation of data from pioneering missions and from related, ground-based, research programs.

This kind of symbiosis between the objectives of the various space agencies and university programs signals a bright future for the overall quest of mankind to 'chart the evolution of the universe and understand its galaxies, stars, planets and life'. The thinking adopted, world wide, to achieve these goals has recognised from the beginning that the pursuit of knowledge is not restricted by national boundaries and, as the new century dawns, common interests, linked with limited global resources, ensures that partnership at an international level will increasingly unite the space agencies, the universities and industry in a program of knowledge advancement based on networking and on the pooling of resources.

CONCLUSION

Consideration of the last forty odd years of unmanned and manned spacecraft exploration allows us to recognise that just as in the early history of the earth living creatures left the water for dry land and, thereafter, spread across the terrestrial surface, what we are presently witnessing is the first faltering attempts of twentieth-century man to leave his environment and seek to both understand, and survive in, a new regime beyond the boundaries of the earth. The significant successes already achieved in this regard and developing plans for the future compel us, however, to now rethink a number of current ideas concerning the relationship of humanity to the cosmos. In today's 'brave new world', increasing space capability raises challenging questions concerning our stewardship, not only of the biosphere of our own, very vulnerable, home planet, but also with regard to the preservation of the integrity of those other locations which will shortly come within reach for human colonisation. As we face in this context a myriad of previously unimagined possibilities, business interests are already eyeing what the first exploratory investigations have found and a goal of 'resource exploitation' of extra-terrestrial locations is becoming a topic for commercial consideration.

In these developing circumstances, an important future role for the universities may well be to provide leadership, based on scientific insight, in the matter of developing an increased level of responsibility not only towards what we plan to do in space in the immediate future, but also towards what we can envision to do over a longer term. We are at a time of new beginnings, and it is proper at this critical moment in world history to reflect that mankind should not only 'go boldly' forward, but that we should also advance towards what is beckoning with due wisdom and reverence.

GENETICS, THE UNIVERSITY AND THE PUBLIC

David McConnell

The relationship between science, the universities and the public is a complex one, needless to say. The dimensions of the topic are great and this essay is short; so I can only touch on some of the difficulties we face in the world of the university, as we try to transmit knowledge of our sciences to the public.

In the first place, I need to state clearly what seems to be the main objective of the university and to show that this objective is quite widely accepted. In 1992, Trinity College celebrating the quarter-centenary of its foundation invited Cardinal Daly to address a congregation of graduates at St Margaret's church, Westminster. Cardinal Daly noted that there are 'many dimensions of meaning in the term *university*. All have the note of

David McConnell studied Genetics at Trinity College Dublin, where he was Auditor of the College Historical Society, Observer *Mace Winner and a Gold Medallist. He obtained his PhD in Biochemistry from the California Institute of Technology and was an Eleanor Roosevelt Fellow in Harvard University. Currently Vice-Provost of Trinity College, he is a Fellow and Professor of Genetics. He was Head of the Department (1987–98), Vice-Provost for Quatercentenary Affairs (1991–92) and Registrar (1997–99). He introduced the technology of genetic engineering to Ireland, he has published extensively in the field of molecular genetics, and was a member of the consortium which sequenced the yeast genome. He is a member of the Royal Irish Academy. His wide-ranging involvement and contributions outside Trinity include: Member of the Irish Council for Science, Technology and Innovation; President, Adelaide Hospital Society; Chairman, Adelaide Hospital Dublin (1988–94); President, Zoological Society of Ireland (1992– 96); Chairman, Fota Wildlife Park (1992–97); Governor, Irish Times Trust (2000–).*

unity and of purposiveness. A university consists of many students and teachers united in a common aim, many disciplines together pursuing a common objective. The common aim, the common objective, is surely the search for truth.'

In a remarkable section of his address, Cardinal Daly drew heavily on Samuel Beckett, and identified with him in a profound way. He quoted from Beckett's *Le depeupleur* (1970), later translated as *The lost ones* (1972), a story about a society of two hundred people enclosed in a cylinder. Among this society, there are searchers who struggle to find a way out, while the non-searchers sit passively against the walls of the cylinder. Knowlson describes 'The lost ones' as one of Beckett's 'strangest, most enigmatic works' that caused critics to argue 'fiercely' whether it is an allegory. Cardinal Daly extolled 'this little people of searchers', seeking the way out, to the sun and the stars. Beckett he says 'remains in a state of austere hopelessness about the arrival of truth, but remains resolutely convinced that the search itself is part of the human condition.'

Cardinal Daly has stated certainly for me, and I believe for us most of us in the world of the university, that we are committed to seeking the truth. He also showed that this is exceptionally difficult. Now more than ever, partly because the acceptance of authority has declined, we are finding it much harder to convince the public of what we believe to be the truth at any given time. We live in an *Age of Uncertainty* (to use the title of J. K. Galbraith's book) in which new ideas and information are being produced in a flood never before equalled in the history of man. This is an age in which the ideas from science are so astonishing as to be at once wonderful, exciting, disturbing and even frightening, but in different measures to different people. It is an age in which a new idea or observation can be transmitted to the entire planet more or less simultaneously in a language which is more or less universally understood. Such information is often contradictory, may carry no real authority but may influence decisions that have a huge impact on the human well-being.

In the case of the sciences, there are universally agreed and effective mechanisms for testing the substance of information and the value of theories – the experimental method. This however has not helped us because the public does not know about this method. At the same time, the public is being deluged with information and misinformation about science. This deluge is profoundly worrisome, all the more so because scientific ideas can have such large practical effects. Truth and the searchers for truth are in danger of being overwhelmed by this torrent of information, much of which is unreliable either by default or design.

GENETICS

Genetics is the science of heredity. In essence, it is the study of biological replication, the property that distinguishes biological from physical systems. Our knowledge of genetics has provoked huge controversies including for example those concerning evolution, eugenics, genetics and racism, Lysenkoism in the Soviet Union, the inheritance of IQ, sociobiology (now related to evolutionary psychology) and genetic engineering. A new one, yet to become widely known to the public, concerns the nature of the human mind. It seems that we are about to discover the reason for 'Descarte's Error' (the distinction between the mind and the body), a revelation which will be strongly related to genetics and surely promises to work more changes in man's outlook on man than any other. Genetics seems to have an exceptional propensity for finding itself in the public eye, surely a victim of its own relevance to our understanding of mankind. It goes to the heart of the matter and must suffer the consequences.

In this essay, I will consider briefly some historical aspects of the major current controversy of genetic engineering. In many ways, the controversy is a reprise of others, illustrating the tensions between a science and the public.

GENETIC ENGINEERING

In 1970, Hamilton Smith (Nobel Prize in Medicine 1978) at Johns Hopkins University in Pittsburgh reported his discovery that Type II restriction enzymes cleaved DNA molecules at specific sequences. The discovery was critical for the development of genetic engineering, the technology that allows us to isolate single genes, alter them and to transfer them between species. The most striking early application of genetic engineering occurred when the human gene for insulin was placed into yeast and the yeast was thus programmed to make human insulin. Prior to 1982, people with diabetes were injected with insulin extracted from pigs. Since then diabetics have been treated with human insulin made in micro-organisms. Genetic engineering is the main technology of biotechnology.

In June 1973, a group of leading American geneticists expressed concern that genetic engineering might produce 'hybrid DNA molecules (which) may prove hazardous to laboratory workers and to the public'. A committee was set up by the

National Academy of Sciences and reported on 18 July 1974. They advised that certain kinds of genetic engineering experiments should be deferred voluntarily until a conference had been held to discuss the 'potential biohazards of (genetically engineered) DNA molecules.' The *Washington Post* in an editorial placed the concerns about genetic engineering in the context of Hiroshima and opined: 'The best we can hope for is that the collective conscience of scientists themselves asserts itself to weigh the risks in each specific instance' and advised against police control.

The scientists did proceed to assess the risks and benefits of genetic engineering. In those early days, there was a moratorium by geneticists across the world, a voluntary agreement to stop genetic engineering. During this pause, there was an intense public debate in the United States, the first ever about whether a newly invented scientific method, genetic engineering, should be used at all. A meeting was organised by Paul Berg in Asilomar in February 1975 and the outcome was reported in an article by Berg, *et. al.*, in *Science* in June 1975. The conference concluded that genetic engineering research should proceed with 'considerable caution', with 'appropriate safeguards, principally biological and physical barriers to contain the newly created organisms', and that 'certain experiments in which the potential risks are of such a serious nature that they ought not to be done ...' The paper laid the basis for regulations that were first enacted by the National Institutes of Health in 1976. Other regulations followed in all OECD countries. In 1978–79 I advised the Board of Trinity College to set up a Genetic Manipulation Safety Committee to supervise my work, pending national regulations. The college adopted the policy of applying the NIH regulations. Today the EU has a set of regulations that have been enacted in Irish law and are supervised by the Environmental Protection Agency.

In summary, the scientists and the regulatory authorities came down on the side of the benefits. They found that the risks are small and not substantially different from the risks of other well-known kinds of biological research, for example microbiology, pharmaceutical science and classical plant breeding. In the last 25 years the regulations have been relaxed considerably, step-by-step as we have learned from experience that genetic engineering does not carry exceptional risks.

But the public debate had the opposite effect to that intended with respect to public confidence. The public was and is not impressed by the leading scientific authorities nor is there widespread confidence in the regulatory authorities. The public could not, and I fear that it still cannot, distinguish those best qualified in the subject from those who know little.

The NIH regulations of 1976 were greeted with some hysteria. An article in the *New York Times* magazine proposed that the Nobel Prize should never be awarded for genetic engineering research, a piece of advice which was not apparently noted in Stockholm. Since 1976 Hamilton Smith, Nathans, Berg, Arber, Milstein, Kohler, Jerne, Levi-Montalcini, Cohen, Tonegawa, Bishop, Varmus, Roberts, Sharp, Lewis, Nuesslein-Volhard, Wieschaus, Prusiner, Gilbert, Sanger, Cech, Altman, Michael Smith and Mullis have received prizes in medicine or chemistry for work which has involved genetic engineering.

The hysteria was impressive. I was at Harvard in 1976–77 working with Wally Gilbert (Nobel Prize in Chemistry 1980) and experienced some of the hiatus. The mayor of Cambridge,

Alfred E. Vellucci, campaigned against genetic engineering and tried to ban it at Harvard and MIT. He was egged on by a group of brilliant, populist scientists (including Jon Beckwith, Luigi Gorini, Jonathan King and Ethan Signer), all members of the radical group called Science for the People, and there were fierce arguments at public meetings. George Wald, who had received his Nobel Prize in 1967 and his wife Ruth Hubbard also of Harvard were completely opposed to genetic engineering. In September 1976, Wald wrote: 'I fear for the future of science as we have known it, for humankind, for life on the earth'.

There was little surprise when nine months later Mayor Vellucci wrote to Handler, President of the National Academy of Sciences (on 16 May 1977), asking him to investigate sightings in New England of a 'strange, orange-eyed creature' and a 'hairy nine foot creature' and check whether these were connected to genetic engineering 'experiments taking place in the New England area'.

The flames were fanned by some extraordinary claims, some regrettably by scientists, about what could be done with genetic engineering. Even then, 25 years ago, the claims for genetic engineering became confused with human cloning, which actually has much less to do with genetic engineering than with embryology. The question of human gene therapy was being raised as early as 1963; gene therapy does have a lot to do with genetic engineering, but is so difficult to realise that it has not been usefully achieved even for one patient many years later. Both human cloning and gene therapy should be and are very tightly regulated – human cloning is illegal and gene therapy trials are carried out under stringent controls.

Charles Thomas of Harvard University wrote an excellent

article in 1977 in which he reviewed what genetic engineering scientists in the genetic engineering debate had said:

> The public is already confused enough on the subject [genetic engineering], and I believe some scientists are as well ... It is a simple fact that the hazards thought to be associated with ... [genetic engineering] are totally conjectural. No organisms of unusual pathogenicity have ever been formed from DNA recombined *in vitro*. And yet the exploitation of this issue has met the special needs of many divergent groups – journalists, television reporters, government bureaucrats, university committees, politically-motivated students and faculty, local and national politicians, and a few scientists ... I believe that you will see that there is some reason to believe the public has been pre-conditioned by incorrect and unwarrantable remarks that have been made by well-known scientists.[1]

He then gives some astonishing examples which if nothing else show that scientists should hesitate before venturing too far from their fields. He applauds Philip Abelson who wrote: 'Talk of dire social implications of laboratory-related genetic engineering is premature and unrealistic'.

So, 23 years after the start of genetic engineering where do we stand? The 'reasonable expectations' for public benefits modestly predicted by Thomas have been wonderfully fulfilled. He said, 'Now, we are on the edge of some very important possibilities, and it would be a genuine tragedy to see this effort halted.' Fortunately, the efforts were not halted and billions of pounds have been invested both publicly and privately in genetic engineering. All of his predictions concerned medical treatment, and this was the most that could be foreseen. Medical science and the pharmaceutical industry have been revolutionised by genetic engineering: human insulin, hepatitis vaccines, triple therapy against AIDS, interferons for use against cancers and multiple sclerosis and so on, have been introduced by genetic engineering.

Thomas made no mention about the impact of genetic engineering either on agriculture or forensic science, both of which have been revolutionised. He could not have predicted that we would have the first draft of the human genome DNA sequence, the genetic code of a human being, by the year 2000. The DNA molecule in human chromosome 22 has been analysed in great detail in a project led by a team at the Sanger Centre at Cambridge. Comprising about 1.5 per cent of the total human DNA, this DNA molecule is more than 30 million units in length and contains at least 545 genes. If this gene density is extrapolated this means that there are between 25,000 and 50,000 genes in man, about 1 per cent of what was expected when Thomas was writing.

On the matter of safety, there has not been a single case of any damage having been done to man or to the environment by genetic engineering, *per se*, in the last 25 years. The car has killed 40 million people since it was invented. William Bateson in 1900 wrote: 'An exact determination of the laws of heredity will probably work more changes in man's outlook in the world and in his powers over nature that any other advances in natural knowledge that can be foreseen'. Our understanding of Mendel's Laws have indeed fulfilled this prediction. It has led to genetic engineering – the largest impact of genetic engineering has been on our understanding of biology.

CONCLUSION

Genetic engineering emerged from the science of genetics in 1970. In Dublin, I began to use the technology in 1971 and I have watched its developments and effects with a mixture of wonder and dismay. In this essay, I have set the science and the technology in the context of the high ideals of the university, the pursuit of truth for the benefit of mankind. The last 25 years have been an extraordinary scientific experience for geneticists and other biologists, who have searched for and found accurate and truthful explanations for many biological phenomena. The huge and joyful intellectual excitement experienced by the biologists has been heavily qualified by the dismay at the public reaction. The greatest casualty has been truth as perceived in the public mind, a fault surely of those who search for truth and those who are responsible for transmitting our understanding of truth, as much as it is a fault of the general members of the public who are going to be affected by it for better or for worse. We can put it this way, that the public has been affected by technology without understanding much if anything about the science that gave rise to it. The present relationship between science and the public is not good. Wolfgang Fruhwald has gone so far as to say: 'A fundamentalist anti-science which comes into existence in many parts of the world could finally destroy the basis for human life'. I agree there is a grave risk that the public turn against both science and technology could be catastrophic. I believe that the only way to avoid this is to reform the teaching of science in schools, so that all students acquire a good appreciation of the history of science and the scientific method, as well as a sound knowledge of our present understanding of the natural world.

REFERENCE

1: Brookhaven Symposium in *Biology*, 29, 348 1977.

Supplying Ireland's Science Graduates for the New Millennium

William Reville

Science has made enormous strides over the past 400 years in furthering our understanding of the natural world. We now know how the world began and how it has evolved. We know how stars and planets are born, and how the natural elements are forged in stars. We understand how our solar system was formed about five billion years ago. We have an adequate theory to explain how life began on earth shortly thereafter and how it evolved into the myriad life forms that now inhabit our planet. Scientific principles have been used to develop a host of new technologies over the past 150 years, and the modern world is entirely dependent on science-based technology.

It would therefore seem safe to conclude that we are living in a scientific age. But, considered from another point of view, it could also be argued that this is not a scientific age. For example, the analytical ways of thinking that have been so productive in science have not been harnessed effectively to illuminate the great debates that shape society. Also, numerous

William Reville holds a BSc and PhD in Biochemistry from University College Dublin. He carried out research on muscle biochemistry as a Fulbright Scholar at Iowa State University from 1973–75 and has worked at University College Cork since 1976 as Director of Electron Microscopy and Senior Lecturer in Biochemistry. Dr Reville is very active in furthering the public understanding of science and writes the weekly 'Science Today' column in The Irish Times.

surveys have shown that, despite its cultural and practical importance, the public understanding and active appreciation of science is low.[1] An example of the low public status of science, one that I will dwell on in this article, is the declining uptake of chemistry and physics by secondary school students in Ireland. If this trend is not reversed, Ireland will soon experience a contraction of our fundamental science base, a debilitating shortage of scientists and engineers, and a slowing down of our booming economy.[2]

The famous Irish-born scientist J. D. Bernal (1901–1971) once summarised society's practical indebtedness to science by saying 'science remains in credit with society to this day on the head of the discovery of electromagnetic induction alone.' It is estimated that over 60 per cent of economic growth in OECD countries is attributable to science-based technology. Our Irish science-based technological economy continues to expand rapidly. However, Ireland is now struggling to produce enough scientists, engineers and technicians annually to fully meet the demand from the expanding economy. *The First Report of the Expert Group on Future Skills Needs*[3] estimated that there will be an annual need for an additional 8,300 engineers, computer scientists and technicians to service the high technology sector of the economy. The annual output in these areas at present is 6,100, a shortfall of 2,200 compared to the projected demand.

These figures highlight two things: (a) the challenge confronting those responsible for national development and, (b) the plentiful job opportunities for young people in science, engineering and technology. The most critical arena in which this challenge must be confronted is our school system where there is a marked contrast between the plentiful jobs available in science, engineering and technology and the muted and declining interest that young people display in science subjects, particularly in physics and chemistry. The numbers of Leaving Certificate students taking biology over much of the last 17 years remained relatively steady at about 50 per cent of the total but have now dropped to 42 per cent, whereas the numbers taking physics have declined from 20 per cent in 1983 to 13.5 per cent today, and those taking chemistry have declined from 21 per cent in 1983 to about 11 per cent today. The situation at second-level has an automatic knock-on effect at third-level. Students who have not taken chemistry or physics at second-level shy away from physical science and engineering degrees.

The government has targeted two areas, Information Technology and Communications (ITC) and Biotechnology, for concentrated development. The ITC sector has a voracious appetite for graduates in computer science. Large numbers of students take third-level courses in this area but the demand for suitably qualified graduates is beginning to outstrip the supply as already described. I will return later to consider the reasons why students take up courses in computer science so much more readily than courses in traditional science subjects, despite the fact that job opportunities are good in all areas. Finally, the reasonable uptake of biology at second- and third-level ensures that, for the time being, we are producing enough graduates in biological sciences to satisfy demand but the recent drop in uptake is worrying. Also, a shortage of graduates will surely arise here if the biotechnology sector takes off as planned.

Young people will not take up careers in science in greater numbers until their interest and enthusiasm for science increases over present levels. The following reasons have been proposed to account for the declining interest in science, particularly in physics and chemistry: – (a) science is not on the primary school curriculum; (b) the Leaving Certificate science curriculum is rather dull, particularly physics and chemistry; (c) physics and chemistry are perceived to be demanding subjects in which it is difficult to attain high points for the CAO system; (d) there is a public perception that jobs are not plentifully available to science graduates (other than to computer scientists) and that jobs in science are modestly remunerated; (e) the scientist is not generally perceived as occupying a high-status niche in society; (f) science has been under attack for some time from certain quarters. I will discuss each of these points in order.

The earlier you introduce science to young people the easier it is to light the spark of interest and enthusiasm that will blossom into a steady flame over the longer term. Interestingly, we knew this in Ireland 100 years ago. In 1897, the Belmore Commission recommended that science be introduced in Irish primary schools and the advice was implemented in 1900. Science remained part of the curriculum until 1934 when it was dropped by our native government – a costly error as it turned out. The good news is that science is now being phased back into the primary school curriculum.

When most Irish people think of their heritage, they think of literature, music, religion and so on. It is not generally appreciated that Ireland also has a proud tradition in science. Table 1 [p. 139] lists a selection of famous Irish scientists who played a prominent role in science over the past 400 years. It is high time that we accorded this heritage the recognition it deserves. In particular, we should teach our young people about their science heritage.

The Leaving Certificate science syllabus, particularly in chemistry and physics, has long been due for revision and a new syllabus has just been introduced. The old physics and chemistry syllabi were long criticised for being dull and lacking that zest that would facilitate the easy sparking of enthusiasm in the young mind. Thus, the chemistry syllabus was criticised for, for example, laying too much emphasis on calculations in the areas of chemical equilibria and bond energies and for a long dull presentation of organic chemistry. The physics syllabus contained only a slight treatment of exciting twentieth-century developments.

Physics, chemistry and biology are practical subjects, i.e., they gain knowledge of the world by physically examining and manipulating it in experiments. You cannot teach those subjects without including a vibrant practical element, but the practical side of Leaving Certificate science has always been underdeveloped. Students naturally love to manipulate scientific apparatus, but, unfortunately, deficiencies in laboratory facilities at second-level have inhibited the educational system from capitalising on this mechanism of sparking interest in young people. Also, no technical support is available in most schools to help busy teachers to set up interesting practical work for the students.

Revised syllabi for Leaving Certificate physics and chemistry have now been introduced in the 2000/2002 cycle. The new curriculum has been welcomed by science educationalists in general. Perceived deficiencies in the old curricula have been dealt with. For example, the organic chemistry section has been given a welcome face-lift and a comprehensive treatment of atomic physics has been introduced in physics. New sections on

Science, Technology and Society (STS) have been introduced in physics and chemistry. And, most importantly, the practical side of the course-work has been formalised with a set list of experiments that must be completed over each two-year cycle. Special funding will be made available to up-grade laboratory facilities. Methods whereby practical laboratory skills can be examined for the Leaving Certificate examination are under investigation. It is most important that this aspect be worked out. Elements of a course that are not examined will not be taken seriously.

It has been generally perceived by students that physics and chemistry are demanding subjects and difficult areas in which to achieve high grades. The statistics also show that the year-to-year consistency of the grading pattern in second-level science is poorer than seen in most other subjects.[4] One of the reasons why biology has been much more popular than physics and chemistry at second-level is because students perceive that examination results in biology are more tightly coupled to effort made. However, more difficult areas of the old physics and chemistry courses have now been softened and new qualitative and interesting sections (STS) have been introduced in the new curricula. The average student will now find it easier to couple good grades with good effort in these two subjects.

High quality science teaching at second-level is hugely important because inspiring teaching can instil a great love for a subject in children. All things considered, teachers have done a good job, but they have laboured under many difficulties, e.g., poor laboratory facilities. Also, because of a shortage of science teachers who majored in physics or chemistry in their degrees, these subjects are increasingly being taught in many schools by teachers who majored in biology. However, new degree programmes are now on offer in DCU and UCC specifically designed to train teachers of physics and chemistry (e.g., a new BSc degree in education for physical sciences, that began October 2000 at UCC, and a new Masters Degree in Science Education that began in October 2000 at UCC offers postgraduate training to existing science teachers to refresh their knowledge and teaching skills).

There is a public perception that jobs are somewhat scarce for graduates in physics or chemistry and, although more plentiful for graduates in biology, are not freely available there either. There is also a public perception that salaries for science graduates are modest. And, finally, the scientist does not rank highly in the public consciousness in terms of social status (this is partly caused by the perception that scientists' salaries are quite modest). In my opinion, this issue of jobs, money and status is the biggest current factor inhibiting the flow of students into science.

The scientist supply problem will be ameliorated by the improvements I described at first- and second-level education in the way science is taught, and by other initiatives to enhance the public understanding and appreciation of science that I will describe later. These educational efforts are essential aids to copper-fasten longer term support for science. However, the scientist supply problem will continue to loom large while present public perceptions regarding jobs, money and status remain unchanged. Students pour freely into third-level courses in areas perceived to offer plentiful employment and good salary prospects, e.g., computer studies, business courses, medicine, law, etc. The scientist supply problem should largely disappear, at least in the short-term, when well-paid jobs are seen to be plentifully available to scientists.

In Table 2 [p. 141] I list my subjective assessment of the public perception, under various headings, of the scientist qualified in a traditional physical or biological discipline, compared with the public perception of a medical doctor, a computer scientist, and a primary teacher. My impressions of public perceptions are very similar to the impressions recorded by O'Kennedy.

If my assessment in Table 2 is anywhere close to correct, it is no wonder that young people display such muted interest in pursuing careers in science. It is interesting in particular to compare public perceptions of the traditional scientist figure (white-coated figure with a test-tube) with the computer scientist. Many people might imagine that a significant proportion of young people would tend to shy away from degrees in physics or chemistry, thinking that these courses are rigorous and intellectually demanding. The coursework for computer science is also rigorous and demanding, but this doesn't inhibit large numbers of young people from opting for this route. I believe that a substantial part of the reason why so many opt for computer studies is that they see a good choice of well-paid jobs at the end of their educational toils. This is not seen clearly in the case of studies in mainline science.

We are told that there is no shortage of attractive and well-paid jobs available to science graduates. Well then, these positions must be aggressively advertised by employers, highlighting in particular the availability of jobs to graduates in physics or chemistry. Indeed one wonders why this has not been done in an effective manner already. The Irish chemical industry recently announced that it is feeling the pinch of the restricted supply of young Irish chemists entering the employment market. It is late in the day to draw public attention to this shortage. The impending supply problem was clearly visible coming down the tracks for many years as the numbers of students taking chemistry steadily declined at second-level. But I don't remember any special campaign by the chemical industry to advertise the attractions of careers in industrial chemistry.

Changing public perceptions regarding availability of well-paid jobs in science will go a long way towards attracting many more young people into science, but, as Table 2 makes clear, there are several other negative perceptions regarding the intrinsic excitement of science and the public status of the scientist that must be changed before we can expect young people in maximal numbers to contemplate science as an attractive career.

The Irish economy has only recently become a big employer of scientists. The image of science as a high-status and exciting profession has yet to become embedded in the public consciousness. The average person has a ready appreciation of the work and the role of traditional professions such as medicine, law, teaching, etc., but would only have a fuzzy idea of the work and the role of a scientist.

Scientists appear on television and radio increasingly often nowadays. However, on average, the public performances of scientists are not well geared to facilitate the most effective communication with the general public. While scientists usually present their messages in simple language, they frequently fail to sufficiently modify the tone of the delivery of the message from the professional tone they use when speaking to colleagues. The provisional nature of the conclusions being presented is often emphasised and the delivery style is emotionally neutral. An impression of dryness and stodginess can easily be created in the public mind – a whole aura can be created of the 'otherness' of science.

Scientists who speak to the public should come across as expert but otherwise ordinary people. While nothing in science is known absolutely for certain, one must be careful not to over-emphasise the provisional nature of scientific conclusions when speaking to the public, who are used to treating knowledge as secure once it passes everyday common sense rules of thumb. And, while it is important to keep emotions out of professional laboratory investigations, the scientist should endeavour to come across to the general public as the warm ordinary person that he/she is. Scientists shouldn't feel they have to hide their feelings when speaking publicly and, for example, a sense of humour is always a welcome lubricant in communication.

Surveys have shown that there is a reasonably high degree of passive interest in science amongst the public and of passive goodwill towards science. This passive public interest can be sparked into active engagement, as evidenced for example by the current surge of interest in popular science writing. Coverage of science is steadily increasing in newspapers, and on radio and television. In particular, *The Irish Times* expends considerable effort in covering science. The Irish government is conscious of the need to foster the public understanding and appreciation of science and has established a Science, Technology and Inno-vation (STI) Awareness programme run by Forfás which does very valuable work.

Recent decades have also seen a sustained attack on science, originating principally from certain academic circles in the humanities and from sections of the green movement.[5 & 6] Irish science has not been subjected to anything like the same intensity of criticism that science in much of the developed world has attracted, but the battle has reached our shores. For example, some critics claim that the knowledge of the natural world that flows from science is no more reliable than knowledge of the world acquired by other methods, e.g., from religious dogma that conflicts with science, or from belief in simple tribal explanations of the world. Others claim that science has become a tool of big business and is being used to irresponsibly exploit the natural resources of the planet.

I am not saying that there is no merit in any argument made against science, because that would be untrue. But many of the arguments frequently made against science are deeply flawed and should be energetically countered. All too often, the reaction from the scientific community to unjustified criticism is to keep the head down and hope it will go away. This is a mistake. When the public witnesses an attack on science that is not answered by scientists it can only conclude that the attack is justified. Spokespersons for science must become much more active in vigorously answering unjustified criticism and much more proactive in presenting the myriad positive aspects of science to the public.

The universities and other third-level colleges, where scientists and engineers are trained, and where most scientific research is done, have a particular responsibility to promote the public awareness, appreciation and understanding of science. This should be done in two ways, internally in the colleges, and externally. Students should be taught how to effectively communicate the gist of scientific ideas to general audiences and should be told that communication with the public is part of their professional role. Third-level research scientists, at least those who have a flair for the media, should use the media to explain their work to the public and to explain scientific discoveries made elsewhere in the world.

Science is intrinsically fascinating and its practical applications underpin our technology-based economy. People are naturally curious and it should not be very difficult, once science is presented properly, to engage most peoples' interest and support. This interest and support are the essential bedrock that must be established to ensure the longer-term good health of science and to anchor it into the public consciousness as a high status and vitally important profession.

Science was woefully underfunded in Ireland until the 1990s, but that situation has now changed dramatically. The ball was set in motion by the 1995 report of The Science, Technology and Innovation Advisory Council on the importance of STI in a modern economy. This was followed by the first White Paper on Irish Science in 1996. The government committed itself to supporting science and funds started to flow. Science is now enjoying great government support in Ireland, but we must be careful how we go.

The government recently targeted information and communications technology and biotechnology as two strategic areas for development and established the Science Foundation of Ireland (SFI) to oversee allocation of £560 million to establish world-class centres of excellence in these areas in Ireland.

The current, and greatly welcomed, support for science is mainly motivated by the realisation of the importance of science-based technology to our economy. But let us not forget the other vitally important reason for supporting science. Science is a hugely important cultural activity – it explains the workings of the natural world and it is well worth doing for this reason alone. A modern society that did not support basic scientific research could not call itself civilised. We must be careful not to drift into a situation where the only scientific proposals deemed worthy of funding are those that promise to quickly produce an economic spin-off. Basic science that produces new knowledge for its own sake is the wellspring of all science, fundamental and applied. If we reduce the wellspring to a trickle, the whole waterway will dry up.

The future is bright. The scientist supply problem will be solved because it has to be solved – our critical dependence on science-based technology ensures this. The only question is – how long will it take to turn the ship around? Certain essentials are already in place. Science is being phased into primary schools and a revised and attractive science curriculum is being introduced into secondary schools. Third-level colleges have shown enormous flexibility in taking in greatly increased student numbers and in devising and offering a wide variety of course options in science and related areas. Irish science is now being funded at a high and unprecedented level. Care must be taken to ensure that this support continues on into the future and that a healthy level of support is maintained for basic as well as for applied research. The print and electronic media are now amenable to covering science on an ongoing basis. They must to be encouraged to do more of this. The onus is mainly on scientists in third-level colleges to supply material for the media, and to become much more proactive in promoting science amongst the general public and in effectively countering unjustified criticisms of science. And last, but perhaps most important of all in the immediate term, employers of scientists must aggress- ively advertise their jobs and must ensure that these jobs are well-paid.

NOTES
1: McDonnell, Martina, 'STI Awareness', in *The Irish Scientist*, Mil- lennium Yearbook, No. 8, p. 8, Ed. Charles Mollan Sampton Ltd., Dublin 2000.
2: Walsh, Edward, 'Science For All', in *Science Education in Crisis*, No. 8, 2000, pp. 11–27, Ed. Carol Power, Royal Dublin Society Seminar Proceedings.
3: *First Report of Expert Groups on Future Skills Needs*, Forfás, December 1998.
4: O'Kennedy, Richard, 'Careers in Life Sciences', in: *Science Education in Crisis*, No. 8, 2000, pp. 79-90. Ed. Carol Power, Royal Dublin Society Seminar Proceedings.
5: Dunbar, Robin, *The Trouble With Science*, Faber and Faber, London 1995.
6: Allaby, Michael, *Facing the Future – The Case for Science*, Bloomsbury, London 1995.

TABLE 1. PROMINENT IRISH PEOPLE IN SCIENCE

Scientiest and their Scientific Work

Robert Boyle (1627 –1691). Born Lismore, Co. Waterford. The 'Father of Chemistry'. Helped dissociate chemistry from alchemy. Studied behaviour of gases. Boyle's Law relates gas pressure to volume.

Francis Beaufort (1774–1857). Born Navan, Co. Meath. Chief mapmaker and hydrographer in British navy. The Beaufort Scale classifies the velocity and force of winds at sea.

Rev. Nicholas Callan (1777–1864). Professor of Natural Philosophy at Maynooth. Pioneering work on electrical phenomena. Developed the induction coil, forerunner of modern voltage transformer.

William Parsons (1800–1867). Third Earl of Rosse, Birr, Co. Offaly. Established the then largest telescope in world at Birr castle in 1845. Showed that many galaxies are spiral shaped.

George Boole (1815–1864). First Professor of Mathematics at Queen's College Cork (now UCC). Invented Boolean Algebra used in design and operation of electronic computers and electronic hardware responsible for modern technology.

William Rowan Hamilton (1805–1865). Born Dublin. Professor of Astronomy TCD, and Royal Astronomer of Ireland. Introduced the terms vector and scalar. Invented methods of quaternions for multiplying vectors in 3-D space, which played seminal role in invention of vector analysis.

George Francis Fitzgerald (1851–1901). Born Dublin. Professor of Natural and Experimental Philosophy, TCD. Proposed that moving bodies contract in direction of motion but the contraction cannot be measured as accompanying rulers shrink in same proportion. This was a significant step towards Einstein's Special Theory of Relatively.

William Thomson, First Baron Kelvin (1824–1907). Born Belfast. Professor Natural Philosophy, Glasgow. Introduced the Kelvin scale – the absolute scale of temperature. His work on conservation of energy led to second Law of Thermodynamics.

Howard Grubb (1844–1931). Born Dublin. World renowned inventor/manufacturer of scientific instruments, mainly telescopes.

George Johnstone Stoney (1826–1911). Born Dun Laoghaire, Co. Dublin. Professor of Natural Philosophy at Queen's College Galway (NUI Galway today). He conceived of and calculated the magnitude of the basic unit of electricity and named it the 'electron'.

J. D. Bernal (1901–1971). Born Nenagh, Co. Tipperary. Developed the technique of modern X-ray crystallography.

Ernest Walton (1903–1997). Professor of Physics TCD. Together with John Cockroft, built the first successful particle accelerator, and in 1932 achieved the first successful transmutation of an atomic nucleus. Shared Nobel Prize in Physics with Cockroft in 1951.

Kathleen Lonsdale (1903–1971). Born Newbridge, Co. Kildare. Professor of Chemistry, University College London. Demonstrated using X-rays that the benzene ring is flat. First woman to be elected to Fellowship of Royal Society (1945).

John Bell (1928–1990). Born Belfast. Worked at CERN Geneva. He developed the set of equations called Bell's Inequalities. He was one of the leading theoretical physicists of twentieth century.

Jocelyn Bell Burnell (1943–). Born Lurgan, Co. Armagh. Professor of Physics, The Open University. Discovered pulsars – rapidly rotating neutron stars. Continues to study various aspects of pulsars.

TABLE 2. COMPARATIVE PUBLIC PERCEPTION

Area of Perception	Medical Doctor	Primary Teacher	Computer Scientist	Physical or Biological Scientist
1: Public perception of role.	Clear	Clear	Somewhat clear	Unclear
2. Status.	Very high	High	Reasonable	Modest
3. Good Career?	Yes	Modest	Yes	Not sure
4. Well paid?	Yes	Not very	Yes	Not very
5. Jobs plentifully available?	Yes	Reasonably	Yes	Not very
6. Helpful to society?	Yes	Yes	Yes	In some cases
7. Potential for self-employment?	Yes	No	Yes	No
8. Long and on-going training and study?	Yes	No	Yes	Yes
9. Exciting and developing?	Yes	No	Yes	Probably
10. Community leaders?	Yes	Yes	No	No
11. Professional/ political 'clout'?	Yes	Yes	No	No

LOOKING BACK, LOOKING FORWARD

Peter Doyle

The year 2000 was the one hundred and fiftieth anniversary of the foundation of The Queen's University of Ireland, an institution now long forgotten and seldom mentioned in Irish university history. The Queen's Colleges were the better-known of these two complementary bodies that still survive today. Despite two changes of name and at least two new charters the basic structure of this university survives basically intact despite the many changes in Irish education in 150 years. This study looks at the National University of Ireland in the light of earlier institutions of higher learning generally and examines the growth of structures determined in the mid-nineteenth century; it also suggests changes that a new century will demand. One area of particular importance is that of the Visitor or similar bodies, then and now.

The Queen's Colleges at Belfast, Cork and Galway are quite well known in Ireland but the university which united these pioneering institutions in a federal system is at best just mentioned. In 1880 it was superseded by The Royal University of Ireland which was basically an expanded body: it was part of the governments' plans to overcome opposition to the 'Godless

Peter Doyle studied in University College Dublin and Vetus Latina Institut, Beuron. He was a Council Member and Clerk of NUI Convocation. Until retirement he was Librarian and Sound Archivist in RTE. Publications on Biblical studies include Proceedings of the Royal Irish Academy, Irish Biblical Association and reviews in Scriptorium.

Colleges', as the Catholic hierarchy of the day described them. Under this new scheme the Catholic University in Dublin became the fourth college and was renamed 'University College Dublin'. Again, in 1908 another reorganisation resulted in the setting-up of 'The National University of Ireland'. In reality, all these universities were one – the structures remained the same as it was in 1850. Within the system, some changes were made to distinguish the newer institutes from the earlier ones. For example, the president of a Queen's College was appointed by the government, a system abandoned in 1908 when the university began to elect its own presidents – initially the incumbents were carried over in Belfast, Cork and Galway. In the Royal University, the Senate had a supervisory, co-ordinating role in setting courses to be studied in the individual colleges. Since 1908, each constituent college has had latitude in deciding the syllabus for itself.

The modern university is used to having considerable choice in how it runs itself. The main contribution of the state is the state grant. In recent years, there has been interference in the matter of fees and measures effecting numbers in individual departments. One example is the places available for the Higher Diploma in Education. However, the incidence of inspections by government is hard to assess: judging by the more recent years the policy has been one of avoidance rather than involvement. A veil of silence has been drawn over this area of activity – inactivity might be a better way to describe it.

A feature of the Irish university system since 1845 has been inspection by Commissioners or a Visitation. Generally, these have been done on an *ad hoc* basis, but a Standing Board of Visitors (as in the case of TCD and Queen's University) would provide a more practical and efficient method of looking into internal university disputes. Past practice illustrates the desirability of maintaining the process in the twenty-first century. The government appointed (and still does) commissioners or Visitors – usually one or more judges – to examine complaints about such matters as misadministration, college-student disputes and even arguments among the staff.

Sir Robert Kane of Queen's College Cork was accused of neglecting his college duties and of altering college council minutes. In 1884, President William Sullivan and the college council in Cork were accused of excessive disciplining of students over activities outside the college. The Visitor broadly upheld the council's view. In 1894, President James Slattery of Cork was alleged to have dictatorially interfered with the rights of the college council. In this case, the president and staff members were criticised by the Visitor. Visitors used to hold public sessions – in one instance the protagonists almost came to blows.

Again, in 1936, there was a visitation in UCC. Officially, it concerned the status of the Dairy Science Institute. President Merriman and the Registrar (Prof. Alfred O'Rahilly) were the main protagonists: the question was 'is the institute a faculty or a department?'. In reality, it was the culmination of ten years of acrimonious disputation involving other college matters. The Visitors met only once – the dispute was quickly resolved.

University College Dublin was the subject of a visitation in 1959 that led to the 1960 University College Dublin Act. The cause of this visitation was apparently irregular appointments in the college that were held to be in breach of the university charter. This time the Visitors met in private.

Where internal problems arise in colleges or universities an

144

independent but internal court of appeal would serve best, since this avoids costly court proceedings. A permanent or standing Visitor, in time, could acquire the necessary knowledge to quickly and efficiently solve apparently intractable difficulties.

Visitations normally result from petitions to the government. The actual number of requests is unknown – only the successful ones are known. However, in 1967 after a well-attended meeting of convocation a petition was sent to the government to investigate the School of Architecture in UCD. This request was turned down. Still more recently the council of convocation was on the point of submitting another petition that arose from a well-publicised dispute between the president and the registrar of University College Cork. Very shortly after this decision was taken a satisfactory resolution was reached in Cork.

The 1997 Universities Act resulted in changes for all the Irish universities and for the National University in particular. Unlike previous legislation, the act regulates the affairs of differing institutes, each with its own character and ethos. It is questionable if such legislation can embrace the particular situation of places as different as Dublin University and the University of Limerick. Each has its own distinctive character. The basic flaw in the 1997 act seems to be a stereotyped approach that underlies the whole act. Within the National University, the constituent colleges had individual charters and had developed individual identities.

When the Universities Bill was published there were many aspects that were criticised, especially the financial ones. Some latitude was shown between the publication of the bill and its passing through the Oireachtas. The minister of the day publicly professed to be open to suggestions. When the final process began the only real freedom opponents of the bill seemed to have was to oppose the legislation. In the Dáil only ministerial amendments were voted through. There were still *lacunae* in the document Seanad Éireann ultimately passed with one major concession by the government: only when defeat faced the minister was there a major concession to Trinity College Dublin after strenuous and eloquent protests by its representatives. TCD got its own act in 2000.

The future of the Irish university system and of NUI in particular should benefit from a study of its past. The complex structure of decision-making in the past in NUI needed an overhaul. The question now is just what changes will be made and which philosophy will lie behind them. The die is cast – the 1997 act is in operation but there was little obvious opposition to it from the leaders of the National University as far as the average graduate could judge. For the outsider the university, represented by its senate, surrendered many points and traditions to the government. The Minister of Education talked about consultations (with whom remains unclear). Apparently, the heads of the Irish universities were involved in discussions with the government as were some university trade unions. At the same time one statutory authority of NUI (Convocation) failed to get a meeting with the minister despite the submission of a memorandum.

In the light of the debate on the 1997 act, some guidelines for the future are needed. The threat of strict government control in every sphere of expenditure seems to have receded, but what has to be stressed is the need for quality in educational standards as opposed to quantity alone. That postgraduate students are not eligible for free education indicates that a real understanding of the role of research is lacking. Only through continuing input into research will the content of undergraduate studies match the needs of contemporary learning and industry to mention but one aspect. Excessive stress on results would be detrimental to worthwhile studies.

Apart from the purely academic aspect, a serious rethink is needed in the approach of university administrators to personal relations in their institutions. Recent years have seen serious disputes between staff and administrations. NUI convocation has consistently advocated a standing board of Visitors that, like its counterpart in Trinity College Dublin and the Queen's University in Belfast, could resolve serious differences from within. This would equally apply to disputes between students and university. This appeals system would avoid damaging and costly recourse to the courts, not to mention the publicity that follows such appeals.

Under the current legislation there is provision for 'internal appeals boards'. The actual composition of these bodies is not specified, and even for the interested graduate no information has yet been made public. Convocation has passed a motion calling for an independent chairman to be appointed to these bodies – an 'internal Visitor'. Only in this way will the 'colleges' avoid the possible accusation that the member or members of these tribunals could be too close to the administration that employs them.

The question of access to third-level education is a topic that the most recent Clancy-Wall report highlighted once again. Clearly, the points system is not perfect but it has been described as the best available. The Dutch 'Weighted Lottery' system has also been advocated. It may be that access methods will be the big topic over the coming decade in Irish third-level education. What will not suffice is a piecemeal, *ad hoc* approach. The government will be a major contributor to the discussion, as should be NUI and other third-level institutes. The senate of the National University has a diminished role since the 1997 legislation but with the experience and expertise at its disposal this is one subject worthy of its consideration. Again, voices have been raised about the suitability of the Leaving Certificate as a determinant of ability for university studies. Perhaps a second look at the Matriculation examination is in order. Within the constituent universities the fact that staff members can be elected to the graduate panel in governing bodies, when adequate representation is now available on 'staff' panels is to be regretted. This imbalance will have to be seriously tackled in the immediate future.

It is all too easy to criticise what happened in the past: looking to the future is the immediate task of the universities but the richness of history provides more than enough guidelines for changes in the future. There are opportunities to be seized, if only the goodwill and experience of today's administrators is fully utilised.

THE UNIVERSITY AND THE EDUCATION OF ARCHITECTS: SOME CONTEMPORARY CHALLENGES

Loughlin Kealy

It may well be the case that learning always has to straddle two ideas of its purpose: that it must serve the needs of today, and that it must address the unknown and uncertain. It is probably a measure of how successful a learning environment becomes, that society will accept the second even as it demands the first. The study of architecture today certainly attempts to straddle these ideas, and does so of necessity, not by choice.

Architecture has been regarded as a 'vocational' profession. Historically, architectural education has evolved from a system of apprenticeship, and the idea that proficiency is achieved through working under tutelage still animates the pedagogy. The dominant arena for learning in the education of the architect is the design studio, where the student works under guidance on projects of developing depth and complexity, leading in time to a design thesis that is the key to graduation. Studio-based learning involves engagement in iterative studies that give rise to the core mental and physical skills of architectural de-

Loughlin Kealy is a graduate of University College Dublin and of the University of California at Berkeley. He is Professor of Architecture at UCD and Head of the School of Architecture. He is a Fellow of the Royal Institute of the Architects of Ireland and a member of the Standing Committee on Architecture of the Heritage Council.

sign. The cliché of 'learning through doing' portrays part of the story, but the intellectual skills involved are subtle and wide-ranging. The student learns to understand the needs that are met through buildings, and to translate these needs into buildings by working through media which stand in the place of material forms and objects – making drawings and physical or digital models as aids to the process. The student's grasp of this tropic process is the key to successful translation into buildings.

The idea of learning skill in design, a skill in conceptual-ising something built through conventionalised images, is distinct from the idea of acquiring knowledge through study. The latter idea is comfortably accommodated within the university setting, the former sometimes less so. Most schools of architect-ure in Europe are not based in univesities; many are based in art colleges or technical institutes. While the two modes of learning are essential and complementary, the pedagogic reality is that they compete for hearts and minds. My contention here is that if architects are to meet contemporary and emerging demands for quality in the built environment, this traditional disjunction has to be transcended. This essay attempts to set out some of the dimensions of the challenge facing architectural education at the present time.

Conventional design practice now faces an escalation in the complexity of design requirements. For example, nowadays, there is a demand that buildings are designed with sustaina-bility in mind, that buildings maximise the use of renewable energies both in their form and the materials they embody, and that their construction and later use is as energy efficient as possible. There is also the requirement that buildings be access-ible to all citizens, so that the old, those accompanied by children, or those with disabilities are not disadvantaged in their use of the building. Meeting this requirement is not a counsel of perfection but a matter of human right, and is reinforced by statutory building regulations. In addition, it is now expected that the buildings of today are designed with a high degree of sensitivity to their context, that they enhance the setting in which they are placed. The conservation of old buildings and their sympathetic re-use is a requirement of culture. The latter is also an ecological imperative, in that existing buildings are an immensely valuable resource to be conserved into the future. These considerations have been overlaid on the architect's established palette of concerns, and as noted, are often now supported by law or regulation. Significant extensions of existing areas of learning are involved here, as well as new areas of knowledge. I will return to this issue later.

An entirely different challenge for architecture is emerging as the urbanisation of the country takes hold and accelerates. The challenges can be presented in terms of two contrasting scenarios.

In the first, we see that the expansion of cities, towns and villages has resulted in the creation of an urban periphery that is both physically and psychologically remote from the established centres of activity. Village extensions that promise to treble or quadruple the base population are commonly proposed, in response to the explosion in household formation. Outlying shopping centres, industrial estates, office parks and extensive tracts of suburban housing are grafted onto larger centres. These developments pose radical questions about the nature of our settlements into the future. Not only is it difficult to reconcile this trend with the imperatives of sustainability and access, the resulting environments challenge the very existence of a public realm, which is a fundamental ingredient of successful urban environments. It is notable that the Green Paper on the Urban Environment, issued by the Commission of the European Communities, puts forward an ecological vision of the city as the dominant human habitat.[1] The paper sees the well-being of the inhabitant as being as dependent on the sense of identity with place as it is on air quality or the management of traffic. Many of the new areas are devoid of a sense of place, they are 'fragments of dislocated space' and as yet, there is little demand that this short-coming be addressed.

The erosion of the public realm is visible also in the built environments of larger towns and cities, where private commercial enclaves and residential gated communities are being created. While they may reflect the need for security and control of the immediate urban environment, they also reflect what Richard Sennett referred to some years ago as 'the fall of public man'.[2] There is a heavy irony in the ongoing privatisation of communal space, even while commerce embraces and exploits the theatricality of urban life, both in its advertising campaigns and in its sponsorship of street events on public occasions. One can of course understand the phenomenon as being consistent with Lefebvre's view of the production of space as being an expression of power relations.[3]

The second scenario is presented by the urban regeneration initiatives now under way. The advent of the Integrated Area Plans offers new potential for architecture and urban design skills by creating a framework within which economic, social and environmental initiatives can be developed. In the case of Dublin city, the introduction of the Luas transit system brings with it the need for careful integration with the existing context. There is clear determination on the part of some local authorities to exploit the opportunities to develop or enhance the public realm.

These contrasting scenarios indicate the scale of opportunity presented by contemporary urban developments. Architecture has always been concerned with public space as well as with the buildings that comprise it. The fact that the focus of attention is on the production of space as much as on the individual building brings this aspect of the discipline to the fore, and with it, the opportunity to contribute to the enhanced quality of the built environment.

And so, to return to where I began, the emergence of these issues brings with it the need to develop architectural education in specific ways. By saying this, I am not simply referring to the fact that new areas of knowledge need to be addressed, since such updating is part of any worthwhile educational programme. Earlier in this essay, I had spoken of the need to develop new skills. Design that successfully addresses the issues discussed above, involves absorbing insights of various groups and being open to the perspectives provided by other disciplines, just as in practice it will involve inter-disciplinary collaboration. Thus, a real challenge will be to integrate this kind of learning into a tightly-knit and intensive course of architectural study. The School of Architecture at UCD has been engaged in a range of exploratory initiatives to see how it can be done. Apart from development of the pedagogy, it is intended to examine the potential for modularisation of courses, to facilitate participation from students of other disciplines.

If the design professions are to sustain their contributions, they also require the capacity to reflect on, and to assess in a systematic way, the experience of past initiatives. Research into the built environment of our towns and cities is underdeveloped, and structured feedback to the design professions virtually unattainable. The scale and rapidity of urban change implies the development of a research capacity that is beyond the scope of individual researchers, or indeed of any one discipline. Specifically, to engage with issues at the requisite level requires initiatives that are inter-disciplinary in nature. To address this need, and in co-operation with Trinity College, UCD has established the Urban Institute, to conduct inter-disciplinary research into the urban environment in a range of programme areas. The Higher Education Authority has supported the institute, and a new building is to be constructed on the UCD Richview campus, adjacent to the School of Architecture and the Department of Urban and Regional Planning and the Department of Environmental Studies. The institute will incorporate a sophisticated data centre, URBIS, which is established with the participation of Ordnance Survey Ireland, the Central Statistics Office and the Environmental Research Bureau. The remit of the institute also includes a commitment to supporting a range of undergraduate and postgraduate teaching initiatives.

In so far as an institution can address the uncertainties of the urban future, some initial moves have been made to create the means of harnessing available intellectual capacities in tackling that task. Architecture and urban design are action-oriented academic disciplines. Inter-disciplinary research will, it is hoped, close the loop between knowledge acquisition and the capacity to shape the built environments of the future.

NOTES

1. *The Green Paper on the Urban Environment*, Commission of the European Communities, Luxembourg, 1990.
2. Sennett, Richard, *The Fall of Public Man*, Norton, New York 1992.
3. Lefebvre, Henri: *The Production of Space*, Oxford University Press, Oxford 1991.

The Editors

Angela Hoey-Heffron, BCL, LLB (NUI) is a solicitor and a member of the Incorporated Law Society of Ireland. She practised for many years in Ireland and South Africa. She is the current Clerk of Convocation of NUI, Chairperson of the Women's Assocation of University College Cork and is a part-time staff member at UCC.

Professor James J. A. Heffron is chairman of Convocation of the National University of Ireland. He obtained the PhD degree in Biochemistry from University College Dublin. He has held research and lectureship positions at the Mayo Clinic and Mayo Graduate School of Medicine, Rochester, MN, USA, University College London, University College Dublin and currently at University College Cork. He is a former dean of the Faculty of Science at UCC. He was awarded the Royal Irish Academy Research Medal for distinguished research on the human disease malignant hyperthermia, elected a member of the Royal Irish Academy and awarded the DSc degree for published work on anaesthetic toxicity and muscle disease by the National University of Ireland. He is a former adviser on the toxicity of chemicals in ambient air to the World Health Organisation's European office.